GOALS

ACTION GUIDE

GOALS ACTION GUIDE

HOW TO GET THE MOST OUT OF YOUR LIFE

ZIG ZIGLAR

Published and distributed by:

SOUND WISDOM
P.O. Box 310
Shippensburg, PA 17257-0310

717-530-2122

info@soundwisdom.com

www.soundwisdom.com

Jacket design by Eileen Rockwell

ISBN 13 TP: 978-1-64095-284-3

ISBN 13 eBook: 978-1-64095-285-0

For Worldwide Distribution, Printed in the U.S.A.

1 2 3 4 5 6 7 8 / 25 24 23 22 21

CONTENTS

INTRODUCTION

ZIG ZIGLAR was one of the most outspoken advocates of goal setting and goal reaching. He discovered that financial or career success very often can be short-lived. Many times people are left with the feeling of dissatisfaction. They arrive at their goals in life and find that they possess many of the things that money buys—but they lack the important aspects of life that money won't buy.

You have important goals to achieve. Maybe there's a personal goal concerning your present relationships. You might have a financial goal to reach or a professional goal concerning the next jump in your career. You also know that setting and reaching those goals requires specific action steps and a concrete plan.

So why don't more people set goals?

Many people have been conditioned to believe that there is no use in setting goals because nothing good will happen to them. They've been told not to expect anything good. They have received negative input, which produces negative output.

Get ready!

You're about to receive plenty of positive input about real world success stories—revealing conclusively that setting goals works! This book contains step-by-step instructions showing you exactly how to set and get whatever goal you desire.

Somebody once said that failure is the line of least resistance. Success occurs when opportunity meets preparation. I believe that is true. You can start receiving the rewards, the dreams, and the desires you've always wanted. Setting goals does work. With Zig Ziglar as your teacher, you can't help but achieve every goal you set.

You will discover:

- How to become a "meaningful specific" rather than a "wondering generality."
- When you put in the effort, you receive the benefits.
- The four basic reasons people don't achieve their goals.
- That you were designed for accomplishment, engineered for success, and endowed with the seeds of greatness.
- The difference between activity and accomplishment.
- How to get the most out of life.

Success is worth the time and effort, but it's not enough to sustain a lifetime at the top. After success, the next step is to move from success to significance. Goals will persuade you to commit to being the best you can be and convince you to recognize and continue to develop what you already have, what you can and will do.

Whether you are just now experiencing Zig Ziglar for the first time or even if you have followed him for years, this book will be a life-changing revelation.

BETWEEN THE GOALPOSTS

Before reading Chapter 1, take a few minutes to seriously consider why you are actually reading this book. Write five reasons you have for reading a book about goals.

1. ____________________
2. ____________________
3. ____________________
4. ____________________
5. ____________________

Right now, what area of your life would benefit the most from having goals and taking steps to reach those goals? Career? Relationships? Financial? Family? Spiritual? Marital? Educational? Other? Write a few sentences why this area of your life is such a concern.

The Introduction states that, "This book contains step-by-step instructions showing you exactly how to set and get whatever goal you desire." Before you get started, are you excited by this statement, skeptical, or ready to prove it right or wrong? Briefly explain your thinking below—then revisit this page after you've finished reading the book and compare your thoughts now and then.

CHAPTER 1

LIFE IS LIKE A CAFETERIA

(FOUR REASONS PEOPLE DON'T SET GOALS)

YEARS ago, a new cafeteria opened here in Dallas. I like to eat in cafeterias because I can choose exactly what I want and I can see what I'm about to eat. So I was excited about this one because it was a new dining source. Every time my wife and I would pass the cafeteria, the line of customers was out the door. Finally, the beautiful day came—no line.

When we walked in, we understood why the line was not out the door—they had snaked it all around inside the place. We were already parked, so we decided to stay. We talked as we walked. When we reached the end of that line and turned a corner, there was another line of about thirty people. We slowly moved forward and when we turned another corner, there was another line of about thirty people.

But this time I could see the food that people were choosing and I made mental notes as to what looked good. *I'll take some of that right now,* I thought. It's important that you make these decisions because I don't care how prodigious your appetite is, no one can eat some of everything in a big cafeteria. So I made some preliminary choices.

Finally, it was my turn to pick up a tray and silverware. As I approached the food, my choices had already been made, so I wasted no time. I asked for some of that and give me some of this and I'll have some of that too. At the end of the counter, I reached into my pocket and pulled out my money. The lady held up her hand and said, "No, you don't pay for it until you get ready to go." I said, "You mean to tell me you're going to let me eat all of this food and not have to pay for it until I'm ready to leave?" She said, "Yeah, that's the way we do it here."

You first put in the effort, then you receive the benefits.

I can't tell you the number of times I've thought about that, because in one sense of the word, that is exactly like life. The cafeteria line is like life. We have an assortment of choices—places to live, things to do, foods to eat, occupations to try. We have an incredible number of choices.

The cafeteria line offers many options, and life is just like that—yet on the other end of the scale. At this new cafeteria we tried, we ate and then we paid. But in the game of life you pay, then you eat. For example, you go to school, you study the lessons, you pass the grade, and you move up to the next grade until you graduate from high school. Then if you go to college, you study your lessons again and get a degree. Then you may go on to graduate school. And finally, after all of that schooling is completed, you accept a position in your profession and work a week, a month, or whatever. Then and only then, after you've done all of those things, you're qualified and you receive the pay you've earned.

You gotta have goals!

Farmers plow the ground and plant the seeds. Then they fertilize and nurse the seeds along, killing insects and watering if there is not enough rain. Finally, the day comes when the farmer can go to the fields and bring in the harvest and take it to the marketplace and cash it in.

That's the way life is—you first put in the effort, then you receive the benefits. You must have goals in life. It is vital that you become a "meaningful specific" rather than a "wandering generality."

PERSONAL GROWTH

As we look at this segment of personal growth, we will discuss *why* we must have goals in life. Most people think very much like this story about the time a wife sent her husband downtown to buy ham. When he returned home, she said, "Honey, you didn't have the end cut off."

"You didn't tell me to."

"Well I thought you knew we always had the end of the ham cut off."

"Why?"

"Well, mother always had the ham cut like that."

"Let's ask her. Mama, why did you cut the end off the ham?" the husband asked his mother-in-law.

"I always had the end of the ham cut off 'cause my mama always did."

Now the couple was curious, so they called Grandma and said, "Grandma, why did you cut the end off of the ham?"

"Because my roaster was too small to fit a full ham," she said.

Grandma had a reason for cutting off the end of the ham. But the question is—did the couple have that same reason? If you don't know why you're doing something, it's best to find out—sooner than later.

REASONS THAT HINDER GOALS

Unfortunately, 97 percent of the people in our society do not have a clearly defined, written-down set of goals for their lives. There are four basic reasons they don't have goals—fear, poor self-image, no buy-in, and don't know how. Let's look at each reason more closely.

More than 90 percent of what is put into our minds daily is of a negative nature.

1. FEAR

The first reason is because of fear—spelled, of course, FEAR, which stands for False Evidence Appearing Real. The average 18-year-old has been told "No" 148,000 times, or "You can't do it." Sadly, 77 percent of our self-talk is negative. J. Allan Petersen, in his book *The Myth of the Greener Grass,* points out that a computer study reveals that more than 90 percent of what is put into our minds daily is of a negative nature. So, a lot of people therefore simply do not set goals based on false evidence.

Because their self-talk appears real, they act accordingly. If it appears real as a practical matter, it has the same impact as if it were real. For example, I could go into any city just about anywhere in the world with nothing but a handkerchief in my hand and I could rob a bank. All I have to do is put the handkerchief across my face, put my finger in my coat pocket, aim it at the teller, and say, "Give me all the money in your cash drawer." The evidence would be false, yet it would appear real, the bank teller would handle my demand as if I had a real gun, and I'd walk out with the money. I might get shot on the way out, but at least the teller would surrender the money.

Many years ago a young Cuban hijacked a plane to Cuba using nothing but a bar of soap. He put the soap bar in a box and told the captain of the aircraft, "This is a bomb. Let's go to Cuba." They went to Cuba. The evidence was false, yet it appeared real.

Fear keeps a lot of people from setting goals.

2. POOR SELF-IMAGE

The second thing that keeps a lot of people from setting goals is their poor self-image. They can't imagine becoming college graduates, getting a superb job, living in a nice home, winning the ideal mate, etc. They can't imagine themselves being financially successful or secure—their image of themselves simply will not let them get there. We perform in accordance with the image or the picture we have planted in our minds. Positive thinking will not work for those who think negatively. Rather, when we have a positive outlook of ourselves, a good self-image, there is no limit to our accomplishments.

One of the most amazing stories that epitomizes what I want to say about this topic is the story of Thom Hartmann who attended one of my all-day seminars in Oklahoma City, Oklahoma. Later, I received a letter from him saying that he attended the seminar because his brother had an extra ticket and it was Thom's day off. There were about fifteen or sixteen hundred other people there and Thom sat in the very center of the audience. He wrote that in the first three minutes he realized he was in the wrong place.

He wrote, "You were in front of the audience saying some wild things like: You can go where you want to go and do what you want to do. You can be like you want to be. And I thought to myself, *Oh brother, that's a bunch of baloney. I've heard guys like you before.* And to be honest, it made me a little uncomfortable, so I looked around for a way for me to easily get out of there in case it got any worse, which is exactly what happened.

"It wasn't three more minutes when you actually had the gall to look at the audience and say, 'God loves you and He wants the best for you.' And I knew that was a bunch of baloney too! Then I *really* looked around for a way to get out, but there I was stuck right in the middle of about sixteen hundred people. There was no way I could get out without creating a disturbance so I looked at my watch and decided to leave at the first break. And that would be the end of that.

"A few minutes later you even made some reference to the fact that we were gonna be dead longer than we were gonna be alive and therefore we needed to be setting some really long-range goals. Then you had the audacity to say to us that we were designed for accomplishment, engineered for success, and endowed with the seeds of greatness.

"When you said that, I looked down and thought to myself, *Well at least he's partially right.* I was looking down at a sixty-three and one-half inch waistline and 407 pounds of bulk. I was coming off a devastating divorce. I had a job only because my employer was my friend and not because I was actually earning the money. I hadn't been to church in many years. I was so broke that every Friday night I was writing a hot check so I could get something to eat.

"I don't really know what it was that you said, Zig, but something rang a bell in my mind and I reached over, got my pen, and started to take notes on my yellow pad. I took notes all day long. When the seminar was over, for the first time in my adult life, I saw a glimmer of hope."

The letter continued, "The next day, the first thing I did was tell my boss that he no longer had just a friend on the payroll. Now he had an employee. I even told him I was going to start carrying my own weight—and at 407 pounds, that represented a pretty substantial statement."

Somebody might resist you once or twice or a dozen times, but when you keep telling them that they are important and they have the ability to do things with their lives, they will eventually believe it.

Thom went to the Oklahoma City University that afternoon and enrolled in a couple of psychology courses. He was already taking courses in history, but switched over so he could learn something about himself. The next day, Thom went to a health studio to do something about his miserable physical condition. Then the following day, he went to a men's clothing store and laid aside about $700 worth of clothes, with a small down payment.

When the owner of the store saw him buying size 47 coats and 39" slacks, he said, "Mr. Hartmann, who are you buying clothes for?" Thom told him he was buying for himself. The owner looked at him like he was crazy; but after a while, Thom did just that.

He wrote, "Somebody might resist you once or twice or a dozen times, but when you keep telling them that they are important and they have the ability to do things with their lives, they will eventually believe it. Your amazing message can go around the world, 24,000 miles, in less than a tenth of a second. Yet sometimes it takes years for it to go that last one eighth of an inch. Your message finally got through to me."

About ten years later, Thom weighs a little over 200 pounds, which is about what he should weigh as he's about six feet, three inches tall and has a very large frame. He teaches a Sunday school class every Sunday. He's in business for himself.

I share this story in such great detail because I believe that when you analyze it, here's a man who was physically bankrupt, spiritually bankrupt, socially bankrupt, and also from a family perspective, he was bankrupt. He was bankrupt in every important area of life. And yet because he became involved in the development of a good self-image, he set goals, and the results were absolutely spectacular.

You have to have goals.

3. NO BUY-IN

The third reason that 97 percent of people don't have goals is basically because they have never really been sold on the importance. That's my prime reason for this book—to sell you on having goals. I'm so confident that you're going to buy in that before you go to bed tonight, you will have started taking the important steps to setting your own goals. I'll even go further than that. If you don't write some of your goals down this very evening, you might as well not go to bed as far as sleep is concerned, because you are not going to go to sleep. If you don't write them down, you're not going to be able to go to sleep.

You will be able to work when you work and play when you play.

You absolutely must have goals. I want to stress that goals work for individuals, for families, for companies, and they work for nations, as well. The basic problem that we face is our self-talk, our thoughts. Most people, when they're busy working on the job, they get to thinking, *I really ought to be spending more time with my family.* And then when they're spending time with their family, they think, *I really ought to be out there working for my family.* And when they're working for their family, their minds go back to being at home, and on and on. Then they complain at work and at home, "I never have time for anything." No wonder—they're always traveling back and forth in their minds!

The truth is, when most people are at work, their mind is at play—and when they're at play, their mind is at work. So they are neither working nor playing; wherever they are, they are just wasting time.

One of the beautiful things about having goals and directions is the fact that you will be able to work when you work and play when you play. I will not suggest that you work harder; as a matter of fact, by the time you finish this book, you will probably end up working less. But when you're on the job, you will be on the job. You will be working infinitely more effectively when you work in this manner and your life will have balance. There is a difference between standard of living and quality of life.

Direction creates time, and motivation creates energy.

Please understand, everybody has goals, but some don't even realize it because they haven't specifically identified them. We need to get more involved so that we know exactly what we are doing and why we're doing it so we can get much better results. You cannot make it in life as a "wandering generality." You must become a "meaningful specific." Many people will go to work tomorrow because that's what they did yesterday. And if that's the reason you're going to go tomorrow, you won't be as good as you were yesterday because now you're two days older and you're no closer to the goal, which you do not have.

Many people complain about the lack of time. But 99 percent of the problem is not lack of time but lack of direction. *Direction creates time, and motivation creates energy.*

Do you remember the last time you had one of *those* days? Maybe it went something like this: You get up early because you have a critically important appointment at 8:30 a.m. and you want to make absolutely certain you get there on time. After you're all spiffed up and ready to go, as you walk out the door, you notice your car has a flat tire. That's the beginning of one of *those* days. You hustle and bustle and sweat and get the tire changed. You change your clothes, clean up, and rush down to your appointment. You get there exactly at the specified time and you see a little note on the door: "Sorry, I was called out of town. I have thought the matter over and have decided I'm not interested. Don't call me, I will call you."

You go to the office and are greeted with a ringing telephone as you walk in. It's your administrative assistant who won't be coming to work that day. You notice it's unusually hot—because the air conditioner had stopped working. A couple of hours later, the plumbing breaks down. It's one thing after another all day long until finally, mercifully, the day ends and you are whipped.

When you return home with scarcely enough energy to walk through the front door, your spouse greets you and says, "Honey, I'm so glad you didn't have to work late because today is when we planned to clean out the garage." *Oh no, not today,* you think, *I'm beat!*

Then the telephone rings and it's a friend inviting you to play golf. "I'll be there in ten minutes!" you say with a burst of energy.

You have plenty of energy to do the things you really want to do. And when you do the things you ought to do when you ought to do them, the day will come when you do the things you want to do when you want to do them.

A lot of people say, "I just don't feel motivated to do anything." Well, they have it backward. When you go ahead and do something, then you will feel motivated to do it. Motivation literally follows the act and motivation creates energy. Start today, right now—write down your goals.

> ✓ When you discipline yourself to do those things you ought to do when you ought to do them, the day will come when you can do the things you want to do when you want to do them.

4. DON'T KNOW HOW

The fourth reason most people don't have goals is basically because they don't know how. I'm going to give you some bad news and some good news. And yes, you're going to get the bad news first. The bad news is this: if you really get involved in this goal-setting process, it will take you somewhere between ten and twenty hours to really assess your goals. If you really have a complex set of goals, it might take you thirty hours to set your goals. That's another reason so many people never record them—it's a tremendous time investment. Now that's the bad news.

Two bits of good news—I can assure you that once you have set your goals properly, you will have created for yourself an additional three to as many as ten hours every week of your life for the rest of your life. Let me say it again, *when you discipline yourself to do those things you ought to do when you ought to do them, the day will come when you can do the things you want to do when you want to do them.* The good news is that having goals will give you an awful lot of time to pursue what really interests you. You will control your time and your activities and your future.

The rest of the good news—when you learn how to set one goal, you know how to set all goals. When you learn how to set a physical goal, you'll also know how to set mental, spiritual, social, family, career, and financial goals because there is a procedure. There is a formula for setting all of them. If you can figure out the answer to 12 times 12, you can also figure out the answer to 2,865 times 9,412—if you know the formula. Likewise, you can use the goal-setting formula for all aspects of your life.

WRITE A BOOK

Let me share a little story. My book, *See You at the Top,* has sold more than two million copies, counting foreign editions. If this book had never sold a single copy, I would still say this is the most profitable thing I have ever done. I'm not only talking about standard of living but also about quality of life when I make that statement. You see, this book you're reading really ought to be entitled, *What I Think You Ought to Do to Get the Most Out of Life.*

As I was writing *See You at the Top,* I realized I was clarifying my thinking about what life was all about. For the first time, I really discovered what I believed was important, and the research uncovered a number of things that I already believed but had never been able to articulate.

I think you should write a book. It doesn't matter if you have it published or not. The act of writing it will be reward enough. I also think the title of your book should be *What I Think You Ought to Do to Get the Most Out of Life.* I want to share information about this because I believe this is a classic example of what goal setting and goal reaching is all about.

The first words I wrote were, "You can go where you want to go. You can do what you want to do. You can be like you want to be." Well, at the time,

I had a 41-inch waistline and I weighed well over 200 pounds; I knew if my audiences were going to believe me and not look at me as a liar or hypocrite, I needed to practice what I was speaking. I had to do something about me.

So, I went to a fitness clinic and they put me through all kinds of tests, took blood, etc. When they finished the examination, the examining physician called me in and said, "Mr. Ziglar, you'll be delighted to know that we've run the figures through the computer, and you, sir, are actually not overweight."

I said, "Well, that's fantastic!"

"However," he said, "according to the computer, you're exactly five and a half inches too short."

So I said, "Well, Doc, that's pretty bad, isn't it?"

He said, "No, actually you're in remarkably good shape for a sixty-six-year-old."

I said, "Doc, I'm forty-six."

He said, "Well, then, you're in awful shape. As a matter of fact, if you were a building, I'd condemn you."

I asked the doctor what I could do and he gave me directions, goals, and steps to take.

When the "opportunity clock" sounded off bright and early the next morning, I rolled out of bed. (Negative people call them "alarm clocks.") I put on my fancy new running outfit, hit the front door, and I ran a block. I did better the next day, though—I ran a block and a mailbox. The next day I ran a block and two mailboxes. One day I ran all the way around the block, came back and woke the whole family and said, "Guess what Dad has done!" I eventually ran a half a mile, then a mile, then a mile and a half, then two, then three, then four, then five. And the weight started coming down from 202 to 165. And my waistline fell to 34 inches.

If you are thinking about losing weight, let me give you a few tips:

- Get a thorough examination from a slender physician. If he or she doesn't believe in the importance of taking care of his or her body, you won't be as motivated.

- If the doctor wants to give you a prescription, don't walk out the door, run out the door. You didn't gain the weight from taking pills, and you won't permanently lose the weight by taking pills.
- If you have a negative doctor, swap out for a positive doctor. Negative doctors basically tell you what you can't eat. They say you can't eat anything you like—but you can have all you want of what you don't like. The thing I loved about my doctor was the fact that he was so positive. He said to me, "Mr. Ziglar, you're going to be delighted to know that you can eat anything you want—and I have prepared a list of what you are going to want."

I can tell you that I can eat lots of chicken, lots of fish, fruits and vegetables, and salads. I can eat on occasion good, lean roast beef. I can eat just about anything that I want to eat now. I believe that a combination of diet and exercise to keep the weight off permanently is the key. One winter I injured my back, for example, and there was a two-month span when I couldn't jog, so I gained eight pounds—my body retains ice cream.

These are the four reasons people don't have goals—fear, poor self-image, no buy-in, and they don't know how. Now let's dispel all of those reasons once and for all!

ACTIVITY OR ACCOMPLISHMENT

When talking about goals, I love the story of Jean Henri Fabre, the great French naturalist.

He conducted a series of experiments with some "Pine Processionary Caterpillars," so named because they follow each other in a procession. He lined them around a flower pot until they formed a never-ending circle. He put some pine needles in the center of the flower pot, which is the food of the procession caterpillar. The caterpillars started going around and round and round. For twenty-four hours a day, seven full days and seven full nights, they went around and round and round until they literally dropped dead from starvation and exhaustion. With an abundance of their favorite food less than six inches away, they starved to death because they confused activity with accomplishment.

It's not abilities—what makes the difference is our thinking and our direction.

A lot of people do exactly the same thing.

I don't know where you live, but I'll tell you something about your town. There are people who are in the same business as yours. Some of them are doing exceptionally well and some of them are not. I don't care what that business is—it's not the location, it's not abilities—what makes the difference is our thinking and our direction.

There are many people who never really have a direction in life. You can see them in every workplace. They come to work and they're almost hyper all day long. They're here and there and everywhere. I mean they're busy, busy, busy. But at the end of the day, they still have a full desk of papers and no evidence that they've accomplished anything—because they really don't have any direction.

The most outstanding example of goal setting that I have ever heard of has to do with the Japanese. In 1950, a war-torn, devastated Japan, a nation that had lost a higher percentage of its young men to war than any nation in the last 100 years, chose a direction. Japan has no real natural resources—no iron ore, no coal, no oil. But in 1950, the leaders of government and business and industry got together and decided to go in a united direction together, declaring that they wanted to become the number-one nation in the world in the production of textiles. During the 1950s they accomplished that goal.

In 1960, the Japanese set the impossible goal to become the number-one nation in the world in the production of steel. In order to do that, they had to build the steel mills and import the iron ore and coal from thousands of miles away. Then they had to manufacture the steel, ship it thousands of miles to its market, and undersell the competition. Impossible! But the Japanese did not look at what they did *not* have—they looked at what they *did* have—a willingness to work, and they worked hard. They reached their goal.

In 1970, the Japanese set another goal. They decided that during this decade, the country would become the number-one nation in the world in the production of automobiles. They missed it by one year. It took them until 1980 when their plant became the largest and number-one producer of automobiles in the world.

In 1980, they set another goal. They said during this decade they would become number one in the production of electronics and computers. And they did exactly that. Goals work whether for an individual, a family, a company, or a nation. I'm absolutely convinced that when we have our goals firmly in place, we will remain strong so we can remain free. Goals absolutely work.

Too many Americans spend more time planning the wedding than they spend planning the marriage.

PLANNING FOR LIFE

I love the story of Sir Edmund Hillary. He was the first man to scale Mount Everest, the tallest mountain in the world. Can you imagine that after he climbed down off the mountain and a reporter had asked, "Tell me, Sir Edmund, how did you climb the tallest mountain in the whole world? How did you do it?" Do you think for one moment he answered, "Well, I was just out walking around one day"? No, of course not. That's absurd, ridiculous. He planned for days, weeks, probably months or even years, setting goals for each stretch of the trek. And yet many people don't plan for any of the important events of their lives.

Too many Americans spend more time planning the wedding than they spend planning the marriage. Too many people spend more time planning how to get the job than they spend on how to become productive and successful in that job.

You have to have goals. Businessman J.C. Penney expressed it this way, "Give me someone with a goal, and I'll give you someone who will make history. But," he said, "Give me someone without a goal and I will give you a stock clerk."

BETWEEN THE GOALPOSTS

Consider these questions seriously—then write the answers and take action.

1. Have you printed or written down your goals?

2. Have you spelled out the details of why you want to reach those goals?

3. Have you identified the obstacles you have to overcome in order to get there? Something stands between what you have and what you want. If there was nothing between you and your goals, then you'd already be there. You have to find out what those obstacles are and choose to overcome each one.

4. Have you spelled out what you need to know to reach your goals?

5. Have you identified the people, the groups, and the organizations you need to work with in order to get there?

6. Have you devised a specific plan of action in order to get there?

7. Finally, have you set a date on each of the goals you want to accomplish?

BEYOND THE GOALPOSTS

Like at a cafeteria, life presents many options and choices. Where to live, what career to pursue, to marry and have children or not, etc. Have you been satisfied with the choices you've made so far in life?

Why or why not?

Have you put in the effort to receive the benefits you expect out of life? For example, if you are an accountant, are you at the level where you want to be in that career field?

If not, what steps can you take today to begin that upward climb?

Do you see yourself as a "meaningful specific" person or a "wandering generality" in life (or at work or at home)?

Define a "meaningful specific" person:

How can you become that person? Write at least ten ways you can absorb that definition into your lifestyle:

On a scale of 1 to 10, how fearful are you about setting goals that affect your career?	
On a scale of 1 to 10, how fearful are you about setting goals that affect your health?	
On a scale of 1 to 10, how fearful are you about setting goals that affect your finances?	
On a scale of 1 to 10, how fearful are you about setting goals that affect your relationships?	
On a scale of 1 to 10, how fearful are you about setting goals that affect your family?	
On a scale of 1 to 10, how fearful are you about setting goals that affect your education?	
On a scale of 1 to 10, how fearful are you about setting goals that affect your faith?	
On a scale of 1 to 10, how fearful are you about setting goals that affect your future?	
How many of those fears are negatively affecting your overall view of daily life?	

Are you willing to dispel, drive out those fears and in return accept a wholesome and positive look at daily life?

What steps will you take today to do so?

Shut your eyes and in your mind's eye, what image of yourself do you see?

Now, check all that came to mind:

- [ ] Happy
- [ ] Tired
- [ ] Clean-cut
- [ ] Shabby
- [ ] Bright-eyed
- [ ] Downcast
- [ ] Confident
- [ ] Shy
- [ ] Hopeful
- [ ] Worried
- [ ] Angry
- [ ] Successful
- [ ] Bold
- [ ] Timid
- [ ] Moving
- [ ] Stagnant

YOU have the power to choose your self-image, whether positive or negative. Have you allowed others to devalue you? Stop. Take a really good look at yourself in the mirror and choose to see all the wonderful possibilities—then place that person permanently in your mind's eye. Check on that YOU daily to keep the right perspective.

Circle one:

How in control are you of your thoughts?

Very Somewhat Not Very

Are you focused or a daydreamer?

Focused Daydreamer Both

Can you concentrate only on work at work, family at home, and exercising at the gym?

Yes Sometimes No

Do you set goals for at work, home, activities?

Yes Sometimes No

Do you write and follow through with to-do lists?

Yes Sometimes No

How good are you at disciplining yourself when it comes to eating healthy food, working toward success, sleeping 6-8 hours a night?

Excellent Okay Not Very Good

Reviewing your circles, do you see a positive or negative pattern of behavior? Think about how your life would change if all the circles reflected a positive, encouraging, optimistic outcome.

If you would write an advice or self-help book, what would the title be?

Would you be writing from your own successful perspective—or would it be about how you wish you could help yourself? Explain.

Have you ever set a physical, mental, spiritual, social, family, career, and/or financial goal? You may or may not know how you reached that goal, but there is a formula to do so. Write what you think you must do to reach every goal you set in life. (Reading Chapter 2 will reveal if you are moving in the right direction.)

CHAPTER 2

NINE STEPS TO SETTING GOALS

THE first chapter was fun. Now we're going to get down to the nitty gritty. This is when we go to work and get into the step-by-step process of setting goals. There are a number of steps involved, which are explained in detail in this chapter and the following chapters.

1. WRITE IT DOWN

Step number one is you *write down* everything you want to be or do or have. You have to *be* before you can *do,* and you have to *do* before you can *have.* The reason you need to write it is simply because writing requires greater concentration, which moves what you write into your subconscious mind more firmly.

I have no way of proving my next statement, but I believe it is true. I've read enough to be convinced that my statement has a considerable amount of validity. I personally am convinced that the greatest benefit that comes from specifically setting goals is that it directs your left brain, which means you are freeing your right brain for the creativity it is designed to do. In freeing your right brain, your left brain is automatically directed toward the realistic goals of life—which is enormously valuable.

Write down everything you want to be or do or have. Put it all down in writing on a sheet of paper entitled "Wild Ideas." (There is space at the end of this chapter for you to write your Wild Ideas.) Now just in case you're sitting there thinking, *Ziglar, it'll take me three days to print down everything I want to be or do or have,* let me assure you that by the end of one hour you will have printed 95 percent of everything you will put on that list at this time. Over the next twenty-four to forty-eight hours, you might add a few more things, but there won't be very many.

> The greatest benefit that comes from specifically setting goals is that it directs your left brain, which means you are freeing your right brain for the creativity it is designed to do.

2. ASK WHY

Then let the list sit for twenty-four to forty-eight hours. At the end of that time, review the list and write one word after each thing you wrote. Write the word "Why." Why do you want to be, do, and have what you wrote? We will spend the rest of this chapter working on why you wrote those things. Are they real goals, real burning desires in your life? Or are they just whims? The real task is finding out what you really want—what will make a positive difference in your life.

3. ELIMINATE

This may sound a bit negative, but we're now going to start eliminating some of what you wrote. I might as well tell you what you already know—you can't always have everything you want to be and do and have. If you can't articulate in one sentence why you ought to be or do or have it, then that thing comes off the list.

For example, I was going over some of my objectives and wrote down some of the things that I want to do this year. First of all, I would like to take a couple of courses in Bible college. I'd like to have a lot more time with my wife, my children, and my grandchildren. I would like to conduct more family seminars. I want to get my daily radio program functioning again. I want a daily newspaper column. I want to play golf five to six days a week. I would like to also be more active in cleaning up some of the programs and advertisements on television. I would like to work in the political arena and get qualified people elected to public office. I would like to spend more time fighting pornography. I want to spend more time with my staff. I want to write at least one book each year. I want to learn how to speak Spanish. I want to become socially involved with my neighbors. I want to read and research a minimum of three and preferably four hours each day. I want to spend at least an hour a day jogging and exercising and taking care of my health. I want to be active in my community civic and social clubs. I want to visit both Russia and China. And I would love to eat Braum's French Chocolate Almond ice cream three times every day.

Say no to the good so I can say yes to the best!

Now to be realistic, not negative, I honestly don't think I can do all those things—I have to say no to the good so I can say yes to the best! We have to determine and then work on the things on our list that are really significant.

When you put too much emphasis on just one or two areas in life, you can become warped.

4. BALANCE

Now you need to balance the list. As you look at your list, determine if it relates to one of these seven areas in your life—physical, mental, spiritual, social, financial, career, or family. Then note that behind each goal on your list. Your goals might be only in one or two or three areas, and that's okay. But let me stress that if you set only one or two goals and are not really serious, the odds are you won't reach that goal even if you follow the procedure. If you happen to reach the goal, I'm not at all certain you'll be very happy when you get there. When you put too much emphasis on just one or two areas in life, you can become warped; for example, you might have a higher standard of living, but where would your quality of life be?

5. EXPLORE

Step number five, we need to explore the basic seven questions. Ask yourself these questions:

1. Will reaching this goal make me happier?

   ____

2. Will reaching this goal make me healthier?

   ____

3. Will reaching this goal make me more prosperous?

   ____

4. Will reaching this goal make me more secure?

   ____

5. Will reaching this goal make me more friends?

   ____

6. Will reaching this goal bring me peace of mind?

7. And if you have a family, will reaching this goal improve my family relationships?

If you cannot answer yes to at least one of those questions, you need to strike those goals off your list. Note: Do not black out or obliterate what you've written down because that goal may not be real for you right now, but a few years from now you might want to revisit it.

6. STRETCH

Number six—we need some goals that are a stretch, goals to make us reach. I love the story of "Gentleman Jim Corbett," the former heavyweight champion of the world. He was out doing his roadwork one morning when he saw a fisherman pulling in big fish and little fish. Corbett noticed him very carefully, and he saw that the fisherman was keeping the little ones and throwing the big ones back into the water.

Being a fisherman himself, Corbett had never seen such conduct, so he ran over and asked the man, "I don't understand. I'm a fisherman and I've never seen anybody keep the little ones and throw back the big ones. Why are you doing that?" The fisherman sadly shook his head. He said, "Man, I hate to do it, but I don't have any choice. I have to throw the big ones back because all I have is just a little, itty-bitty frying pan at home."

Now before you laugh too loudly, let me point out he's talking about you and me. So many times we get the big goal, the big dream, the big idea, and no sooner do we get it than we say, "Oh no, Lord, don't give me such a big one...all I have is just a little, itty-bitty frying pan. Besides, somebody else probably already thought about it, so just give me one of those little ones."

Go as far as you can see, and then when you get there, you will always be able to see farther.

LONG-RANGE GOALS

Friend, we have to have some big goals to make us stretch and use the ability inside us; some goals must be long-range. If there are detours along the way, that's okay. Just readjust your direction. I hold on to the phrase, "Don't change your objective; just change your direction to reach it." This is after you have really set a definite goal or objective.

If you have a long-range goal, don't forget that before you reach it there will be trouble in front of you. No matter the goal, things will happen in life that you can't control. But you must treat those *temporary* setbacks like a pebble on the beach. If you don't have long-range goals, setbacks will become as big as the whole ocean front. The rule is simple—*go as far as you can see, and then when you get there, you will always be able to see farther.*

You have to have some long-range goals, and you have to have some small, daily goals—the nitty gritty things of life. Everybody loves the big dream—the excitement of dreaming about a trip to Honolulu or a trip around the world, dreaming about building a mansion, dreaming about having the first million and then the second million, and so forth. But the reality is, in order for the big things to happen, you have to accomplish the little goals designated along the way. Also, some goals need to be ongoing.

ONGOING GOALS

What's an ongoing goal? Building up your *self-image* is an ongoing goal because even after you're an adult, even after you're forty or fifty years of age, you can have a devastating experience. For example, people's self-image can be destroyed when they have been on the job for thirty years and then new management summarily dismisses them. They can't find employment for the next six months or a year or two years. The impact can be devastating. Or maybe their mate walks out on them. That can be a devastating blow to their self-image.

Our *health* is an ongoing goal. I routinely work on keeping a healthy body. Exercising is something I do on an ongoing basis. *Spiritual* goals are ongoing. *Relationship* goals are ongoing goals. And most people need ongoing *financial* goals.

7. NEGATIVITY CHECK

Number seven is to check for negativity. Goals can be negative if they are too big. If a goal is out of reach, that's one thing. But if it is out of sight, that's something else. Unrealistic expectations are the very seedbed of depression. For example, after speaking in Detroit a number of years ago, a young man, twenty-four years of age, came to me all excited and said, "You got me really excited and I'm gonna make a million dollars this year!"

This was a young man whom I happened to know did not have the $2,500 for the franchise fee on the product that I was teaching and training for that particular company on that day. He had been working for four years, yet he was unable to save $2,500. But in the next twelve months he thinks he's going to earn a million dollars. Now that's crazy—his presumption had no foundation in fact or reason.

Your goal could also be negative if it is out of your field. Speaking about goals in Salt Lake City several years ago, a young man, thirty years of age, came to me after the session. He was about five feet seven inches tall and weighed about 210 pounds. He announced to me that his goal was to be the light heavyweight boxing champion of the world. I asked him how much experience he had.

"Well," he said, "last Saturday my brother-in-law and I were out in the backyard boxing around and you can't believe how easily I handled him!"

I asked, "How much experience have either of you had in boxing?" Well, neither of them had had any experience. Now that was a guy headed for the cemetery. He would get killed in the ring with a professional. There's no question about it. That goal was completely out of his field. A goal can be negative if it is completely out of your field of interest or expertise.

The third reason a goal can be negative is if you have to depend on luck in order to get there. If it's "pluck"—spirited and determined courage—that's required, you have a chance. But luck? No way.

Now remember, what we're doing is keeping the main thing, the main thing. We're gradually working on determining what we really want.

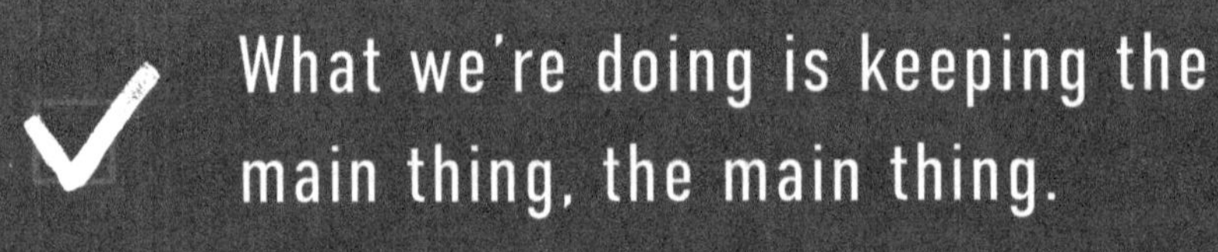

8. ASK FIVE QUESTIONS

Step number eight is to ask ourselves five questions. The first question: *Is it really my goal?* There are a lot of doctors, lawyers, preachers, plumbers, and all kinds of professions who are not as good as they could be because they did not pursue their own objectives. Their parents, grandparents, preachers, professors, or friends at some point may have said something like, "You know, you're good at that! You should be a..." and somebody else basically ended up setting their goals.

There are occasions when two guys graduate from school together and one gets a job first at the nearby factory or with a company, and he tells the other guy, "I have a great job with benefits that are out of this world. It's a nice environment to work in, too. You should apply." And a lot of times, with no more thought than that, the other guy makes a career choice. Then five and sometimes ten years later, they are both still there—and stopping by the bar too frequently on the way home. They're bored to death with what they're doing. They took the first job that came along. Figure out *your* goal, then pursue it.

The second question: *Is this goal morally right and fair to everyone concerned?* The idea of abusing others and walking over them, taking advantage of them to achieve your objectives simply is not valid in this competitive world of ours today. We have to work in cooperation with others. Remember, even the Lone Ranger had a buddy, and he worked with his buddy. Your goal must be morally right and fair to everyone concerned.

Number three—ask yourself, *Will this goal take me closer to or further from my major objective?* Every decision you make should be weighed against how much closer you will be to achieving your goal. That includes every purchase as well.

One summer my wife and I went to Japan to look at their schools and factories. Then we stopped in Hong Kong to do our bit for the local economy, then we flew on to Malaysia where I had a seminar, then on we traveled to New Zealand and Australia where I had six seminars.

Will this goal take me closer to or further from my major objective?

Before the trip, our son, who was a senior in college at that time but would graduate before we made the trip, told us he'd like to go along with us. I said, "Well, son, have you asked yourself the two questions? Have you asked if it is morally right and fair to everyone concerned?"

"Since you'll have to pay for it, Dad, that's a question you're going to have to answer."

I said, "That's fair enough. Now how about question number two. Will it take me closer to or further from my major objective in life?"

My son's major objective was to become a PGA touring pro. We think he has the ability. His pro thinks he's got the swing. I think he has the temperament. But that's still a big step, and the odds are prohibitive—but that's his major objective. So I added, "Will it take you closer to or further from your major objective when you are off the practice course for one solid month and delay your career?"

He said, "I don't think I'll go."

Well, we weren't going to take him anyway, but it was so much better for him to make that decision for himself than for me to say, "No, you can't go." He's much happier with the outcome because he made the decision.

The fourth question: *Can I emotionally commit myself to start and finish this project?* Friend, unless you get emotionally involved with your commitment to the project or goal, nothing is really going to happen. We're not logical people; we are emotional people. We must seriously consider if we can or cannot emotionally commit ourselves to start and finish each project that will get us to our goal.

And the last question: *Can I see myself reaching this goal?* When my goal was to lose weight, I had a picture of a guy wearing jockey shorts hanging on my bathroom mirror. I saw that picture about ten thousand times during that ten-month period of time. Every time I went into the bathroom, there he was. I had a clear vision of exactly how I wanted to look. Now that's important. *You need to be able to visualize.*

9. CHOOSE TOP 4

The ninth step in the process is to work your list down to just four goals of what you want to do, be, and have. Most people can really only give complete effort to about four goals at the same time. You might still have ten or fifteen things on your list, but you need to focus on no more than four. Look carefully over the list again. Maybe one you can't really get started on now. Maybe another one isn't quite as important as another one. Work it down until you get to seven or eight.

Now here's the way you work the list of goals all the way down to four.

When going through this process, first of all you need to *take inventory of where you are.* For example, on Thursday afternoon at 5:20 when I get aboard an aircraft headed to St. Louis, if the captain of the aircraft thinks that we're in Houston, I'm not going to make it to St. Louis. The pilot needs to know we're in Dallas, Texas, if the passengers are going to end up in St. Louis. Likewise, you need to know where you are if you're going to reach your objective. You need to work through the whole goal process.

Next in this process, step two is to *write down the goal.* Now I'm going to share with you the exact process I went through in my weight-loss situation discussed in the previous chapter. I first identified my goal, which was to weigh 165 pounds and have a 34-inch waistline. July 1, 1974 was the date when I expected to reach that objective. I identified it and I wrote it down. Normally you can't put the time on a lot of your goals until you've gone through the entire process. I only put the date on it after I had gone through the process, but that was the objective that I had.

Step Three: What are the *benefits* from reaching this goal? One of the major reasons people can't quit smoking or drinking or lose weight or whatever is because they emphasize the negative. The most important thing you can do in this goal-setting process is to emphasize, "What's in it for me?" That might sound selfish, but it is *your* goal that you're working for. And remember, you've asked the proper question beforehand—is it morally right and fair to everyone concerned? So, it's not a question of you looking after yourself to the detriment of everybody else.

What were my benefits for losing weight? First of all, the odds are strong that I'm going to look better. The second benefit, everything else being equal, I will live longer. The third benefit, I will have more energy and will feel better. The fourth benefit, I will undoubtedly be sick less. Historically speaking, those benefits worked out to be 100 percent true. Except when I had a couple of surgeries, which had nothing to do with my diet and exercise, I had gone fifteen years without missing one day of work. When you take care of your physical health, good things are going to happen that are in your best interests.

Step Four: What are the *obstacles* and mountains I have to climb to reach this goal? What do I have to do to lose this weight? Well, I've always been on a see-food diet. That means when I'd see food, I'd eat it. But I really was a light eater—meaning when it got light out, I started eating. I never saw food I didn't like—I made friends with all of it. The only things I don't like are green olives, anchovies, pimento cheese, and caviar. And I could eat a well-balanced meal without any one of those, I guarantee you.

So what were my obstacles? One obstacle is that I like food. Another obstacle is that my schedule is very irregular and I want to eat at odd times. When I present a three or four-hour seminar, I burn a lot of energy. When I finish a seminar, I really want to eat a big meal, but instead I eat a piece of fruit. I had to deal with the obstacles in front of me; those were two of them. Another obstacle was my tendency to eat entirely too fast. I'm a shovel eater—I just shovel it in.

Step Five: What other *skills or knowledge is required* to reach this goal of losing weight? All I really needed to know is about diet and exercise. I only needed to know two things, so I wrote that down—diet and exercise.

Many times we need somebody to work with and teach us.

Step Six: Who are the individuals, groups, companies, and organizations *to work with* to reach this goal? First of all I had to work with my wife. I had to coordinate my eating and my jogging to fit within the family plan. Second, I had to work with my administrative assistant as she's the one who schedules my activities. I'm frequently invited to dinner when I present seminars and I accept only if I have time between the seminar and the dinner to jog.

Now when you start talking about people who work with you to reach your goal, let me remind you that somebody taught Albert Einstein that two plus two is four. Let me also remind you that somebody taught Joe Lewis how to hold his guard up. Somebody taught Mozart the scale. Somebody taught Sir Edmund Hillary how to climb the little hill before he ever got to Mount Everest. Many times we need somebody to work with and teach us.

Step Seven: What was my *plan of action* to reach this goal? This is the step that really gets into the nitty gritty. This is where we really find out if we are serious about reaching the goal. What was my plan of action? First, I decided because of my love for breads and sweets, I wasn't going to eliminate them completely from my diet. So, I became a once-a-week eater of desserts. Every Sunday after church I would make a beeline for the Braum's French Chocolate Almond place.

Now as you probably well know, some ice cream scoopers are better scoopers than other scoopers. So I'd wait in line until a good scooper came up, and then I'd turn around and say, "I'll take a double dip of that good ole Braum's French Chocolate Almond ice cream." I couldn't wait until Sunday afternoon to go to the ice cream place. That was *part* of my plan of action.

The other part of my plan of action was to travel with a grapefruit. That's not the best traveling companion you can find, but I discovered that a large grapefruit has only about 110 calories. Eating it would take the edge off of my appetite and I would go to bed at least reasonably satisfied.

The third part of my action plan was to put my fork down after every bite. I would reach over and pick up a fork-full of food, put it in my mouth, and then place the fork onto my plate. I forced myself to think about every bite of food. This step slowed down my eating dramatically. Then as soon as

I finished eating, I would go to the bathroom and brush my teeth, signaling to myself that the meal was over.

Another plan of action I had was to eliminate the bread and dessert from airplane meals. In those days I was eating about six meals each week on an airplane. When the tray with the entrée, bread, and dessert was brought to me, I would immediately pick up the bread and the dessert and give it back to the flight attendant who brought it to me. Problem solved.

IT'S ALL IN THE DETAILS

You might think that is an awful lot of detail and you're not sure you want to know that much about my plan of action, but let me tell you, when you go through the whole process and you start developing *your* plan of action, you will discover that some goals need that level of detail—and that other goals are simply not practical for you at this time. Doesn't it make more sense to eliminate a goal after working on it for an hour and a half than it is to strive with it for six months and then give up in frustration?

A goal properly set is halfway reached.

I want to get you zeroed in on what is important *right now* for you to work on that will let you accomplish your objectives. Then the details are absolutely critical.

I can look you right in the eye and tell you that since December 1, 1986, with the exception of three days last June and one day last February, I have worked on my goals every single day. I can tell you where I've been, what I've been doing, what I've been working on, and what I've accomplished.

I've always been fairly conscientious about my goals; I've been working toward them for years. I can tell you without any mental reservation, when you start doing it this way, when each evening you take certain steps, once you have those goals set, I can tell you that you can accomplish dramatically more than you've been accomplishing in the past.

Remember, friend, a goal properly set is halfway reached.

BETWEEN THE GOALPOSTS

1. Have you printed—written on paper, not your computer or iPad—everything you want to be or do or have? If not, do it now, here:

2. Now ask yourself "why" you listed those certain goals. Are they whims or sincere desires that will improve your life? Label each one W for Whim or D for Desire.

3. Now you need to eliminate some goals after asking yourself about each:

- Will reaching this goal make me happier?

- Will reaching this goal make me healthier?
- Will reaching this goal make me more prosperous?
- Will reaching this goal make me more secure?
- Will reaching this goal make me more friends?
- Will reaching this goal bring me peace of mind?
- And if you have a family, will reaching this goal improve my family relationships?

Cross off the goals in pencil, as they may be goals you want to revisit later in your life.

4. List your long-range goals and your ongoing goals according to the descriptions of each in the chapter.

5. Of the goals that remain, ask yourself the following five questions:

- Is this really *my* goal?
- Is this goal morally right and fair to everyone concerned?
- Will this goal take me closer to or further from my major objective?
- Can I emotionally commit myself to start and finish this project?
- Can I see myself reaching this goal?

6. Considering all the steps taken to list and then eliminate your goals, choose four goals that you feel you can and want to achieve:

1) ____________________

2) ____________________

3) ____________________

4) ____________________

Now write down the answers to these questions for each of the four goals:

- What benefits will I gain?

____

____

- What are the obstacles?

____

____

- What knowledge or skills do I need?

____

____

- Who else must be involved?

____

____

- What is my plan of action?

____

____

YOUR WILD IDEAS

BEYOND THE GOALPOSTS

Step 1 is to write your goal. Is it your habit to write things down so you don't forget what you need to do? If so, great! If not, it's a habit worth making.

Do you agree that writing requires greater concentration than just thinking about something?

Do you normally write on paper with a pen, or electronically on your phone or tablet?

Why do you write, and what do you usually write about?

Are you willing to take the time to write your career and/or life goals?

Do you consider yourself controlled more by the right side of your brain (creative/emotion) or your left brain (logical/analytical)?

Do you believe that when you write your goals it allows you to think creatively about new and innovative ideas and aspirations? Or do you write logically just to keep you from forgetting something you need to do? If the later, how hard will it be for you to write creatively and emotionally? Are you willing to try? Why?

Step 2 is to ask why. After you wrote your "wild ideas" list, did you take time to ask yourself why you want to be, do, and have what you wrote? If not, do so now:

Now write BD after your Burning Desires ideas. Write RG after your Real Goals. Write W after your Whims. Write PD after the ones that will make a positive difference in your life. Be honest with yourself—and you are on your way to creating some exciting journeys in life!

Step 3 is to eliminate what you wrote. Cross off the list all the "Whims." For example, if you wrote I want to live happily ever after in Hawaii, that's probably a whim. (Although, if you are serious about a surfboard building business and have a burning desire and real goals to make that happen, it's not a whim.) How many whims have you crossed off the list?

How many things do you have remaining on your list? ________ How many are unrealistic? ________ How many are most significant and will impact positively on your life and the lives of your loved ones? ________

Step 4 is balance. A balanced life means equal weight in the following areas. So the total is 100 percent, insert the number for each area that reflects your emphases in life currently:

Physical: ________ percent

Mental: ________ percent

Spiritual: ________ percent

Social: ________ percent

Financial: ________ percent

Career: ________ percent

Family: ________ percent

Too much emphasis in one area can warp another area or areas. Do you see a problem? Explain

____

____

____

____

Step 5 is to explore your motivations. Did you ask and answer the questions in the chapter? ________ How many goals did you mark off your list as a result? ________ How many things remain on your list? ________

Step 6 is to figure out which goals are going to be a stretch to achieve. Don't be afraid to step out in faith to reach a goal or burning desire if you have a deep down knowing that you can do it.

How many long-range goals do you have? ________

Write them:

____

____

____

____

____

____

____

____

How many ongoing goals? ________

Write them:

Step 7 is a negativity check. Large goals can become daunting and unrealistic expectations can lead to depression. Write a few things you would like to do or be that you know deep down are not realistic:

Delete these from your list if you haven't already.

Step 8 is to ask yourself five questions.

Are these goals my goals or someone else's? ____________________

Are my goals moral, right, and fair? ____________________

Will my goals lead me to my ultimate goal? ____________________

Am I emotionally committed to reaching each of the goals? ____________________

Do I actually see myself reaching my goals? ____________________

Step 9 is to choose the top four remaining on your "wild ideas" list. Write your ***top four goals*** of what you want to do, be, and have:

____

____

____

____

Write the ***benefit of each*** of the four goals:

____

____

____

____

Write anything that may prevent you from reaching any of your goals:

What skills or knowledge is necessary to reach these goals?

Who do you need to work with to reach the goals?

Write your plan of action for each:

How committed are you to completing these steps to reach the four goals you have chosen as the ones to accomplish?

Very Committed	Mostly Committed	Somewhat Committed	Burnt Out Already

CHAPTER 3

DAY-BY-DAY FORMULA

One person with a commitment is worth more than one hundred who only have an interest. —**Mary Crawley**

AFTER you have *set* your goals, there is a formula you can use to *reach* your goals. This chapter gives you ways you can get closer and closer to your goals—day by day. First of all, I'm convinced that people who make commitments to reach their goals are the ones who are going to reach them.

People who make commitments to reach their goals are the ones who are going to reach them.

STEP 1: COMMITMENT

A number of years ago, a young coach at the University of South Carolina was fired after his first season on his first job. Not only did the head coach say, "There's no more for you here," but he also advised him to get out of coaching and told the young man, "Let's face it, you just don't have it."

But the young coach had set his goal; he had made a commitment. He had said, "Someday I'm going to coach at the University of Notre Dame." Ohio State gave him a chance, and he was an assistant there for a couple of years. Then William and Mary College called him and he was the head coach. North Carolina State University called him and he was there for four years and they had the best one-loss record the team had ever had.

From there he went into the pros and coached the New York Jets for a season, but he really missed coaching young men and helping to mold their character. The University of Arkansas called him and he had a phenomenally successful career there. He built the best one-loss record they ever had. Before he took the team to play the University of Oklahoma at the Orange Bowl, the media had speculated that it would be a mismatch, that Oklahoma simply was too powerful. To compound the problem, three offensive players, the entire offense of that Arkansas team, were caught with a woman in the room. There was an investigation and it was discovered that it was absolutely true—and the coach immediately dismissed all three players.

The media again speculated that he should decline the invitation to the Orange Bowl and let somebody else accept the invitation who would be a worthy opponent for the Oklahoma team. But this coach was a committed man. He looked at the team he had left and didn't worry about what he did *not* have. He accentuated the positive and developed a specific game plan. The rest is history—they won the game by a wide margin.

He left the University of Arkansas and became the head coach at the University of Minnesota. When he accepted the Minnesota assignment, he said that he would take the assignment provided they would give him one out with two conditions—if he takes the Minnesota team to a bowl within two years and if the University of Notre Dame called him to be their head coach. He was setting goals again. Well, two years later, the University of Minnesota was invited to play in a bowl game and the University of Notre Dame called him to be their head coach.

Now the interesting thing is this. The Notre Dame leadership knew this coach was someone they wanted the day he dismissed those three players from his team when he was at the University of Arkansas several years earlier. They had made their decision the day that happened, saying here is a man who is interested in building character and developing leaders. This is the man we want to be our coach. The next time we have an opening for the head coach at Notre Dame University, we'll be calling him. I'm obviously talking about Lou Holtz.

I happen to know Lou quite well. He said that there never was any doubt in his mind about dismissing those players. It was the right thing to do. What I'm saying is that *when you have a solid base with a solid commitment and solid objectives, you have a much better chance of reaching your goal.* But it takes commitment.

> When you have a solid base with a solid commitment and solid objectives, you have a much better chance of reaching your goal.

1. MY COMMITMENT

When I wrote my book *See You at the Top,* the first words I wrote were, as mentioned previously, "You can go where you want to go. You can do what you want to do. You can be like you want to be." When I worked on the goal segment in the book, I wrote that I weighed 165 pounds and I had a 34-inch waistline. The moment I wrote that, I actually had a 41-inch waistline and weighed over 200 pounds. I had made a commitment to get that weight off, and I put it in print that I would do it.

Not only that, but when I had finished the first summation of the book and had written the chapter headings and a little bit of the content, I sent it to three major publishers knowing that they would really be excited to get this manuscript draft from this unknown author. I knew that in all reality those three publishers would get in a bidding war and they would fight each other about who was going to have the honor of publishing my book.

You can imagine my shock, chagrin, and disappointment when I received letters from all three saying they didn't think the book was going to sell.

Well, I knew better. But it's one thing for me to say to a publisher, "How about you publish it and if its sells, you don't have to pay me any royalties. And if it doesn't sell, well gee, I'm sure sorry about that." It's one thing for me to get them to invest their money; but the question was, did I really believe the philosophy I had been talking about all over the country? Did I really believe that the book would sell? I had to make a decision.

I decided to publish it myself. A friend of mine said that if I would sell 25,000 copies, I'd have a bestseller. That prospect appealed to me enormously. I decided to print 25,000 copies. Now I don't know what you know about book publishing, but let me tell you two very basic facts. First of all, the first copy will cost you more than the next 24,999 copies. The second thing is that those 24,999 copies cost a whole bunch of money, especially if you don't have it. I decided, though, that I believed the book would sell. I decided to go ahead and publish that book. That is commitment.

Can you imagine me with a warehouse full of books saying I weighed 165 pounds and I come waddling out at 202? I would still have a warehouse full of books. Let me tell you what human nature is like. If I lie to you one time about one thing, from then on you're going to have a question mark after everything I tell you. Likewise, if you lie to me one time about one thing and I know it is a deliberate lie, I'll put a question mark after everything you tell me after that. Had I not lost that weight, I could well imagine a lot of people reading my book where I wrote I weighed 165 pounds and yet they would look at me and see 202. I have no doubt they would all wonder what else I lied about. So I lost the weight, true to my commitment.

Friend, you must commit yourself to your goal if you expect to reach your goal.

STEP 2: ACCOUNTABILITY

The next step is to keep a daily, detailed accountability record. I can say it four thousand different ways, but the bottom line is, unless you discipline yourself on a daily basis to keep records of what you do, the chances are very strong that you are not going to reach your goals. You will simply lose sight of what you say is extremely important to you. Each evening is when you write your plans for the next day.

Peter Drucker made an observation about time management and conducted presentations entitled "Know Thy Time." He said, "Time is the scarcest resource, and unless it is managed, nothing else can be managed." And, "If you want to improve how you manage time, stop doing what doesn't need to be done!"

Now remember, you're only working on four to six things on your goal list. So once each week you need to look at those goals and decide which one or ones you will work on that week. During the course of the week in my performance planner, if I don't do anything at all that day on that goal, I write the word "nothing" in red ink. At the end of the week, I can glance quickly and instantly know if I'm headed for trouble. If miss it one day, that's not a big deal. If I miss it two days, maybe I better start exploring because I'm headed for some trouble. Get serious about this daily, detailed accountability task. It will take you only about ten minutes each evening.

If you're going to reach your goals, you have to start with a solid foundation, which is comprised of honesty, character, integrity, loyalty, trust, love, and faith or trust.

STEP 3: SOLID FOUNDATION

If you're going to reach your goals, you have to start with a solid foundation, which is comprised of honesty, character, integrity, loyalty, trust, love, and faith or trust. When I was in Calgary, Canada, I had the opportunity to go up the Calgary Tower to have dinner. When we stepped into the elevator, a recording came on saying that the tower is 626 feet high. I could only visualize that height by thinking of two football fields and then 26 additional feet. I can relate to that, so that was the picture I had in my mind. Then the recording said that the structure weighs 13,000 tons and 7,000 of those tons are underground. When you have a foundation like that, you can go 626 feet up in the air or even higher.

In any city in the world, a good engineer can look at a hole in the ground and tell you how wide, how broad, and how tall the future building is going to be—just by looking at the kind of foundation it is going to have.

I don't care whether your future lies in athletics, entertainment, music, sales, education, law, or medicine. It makes zero difference what your future is and what your goals are. But I can tell you this for certain, if you have a solid foundation to build on, the odds are dramatically increased that you will reach your goals. These principles work for a nation, family, individuals, and companies. You have to have a solid foundation.

Mortimer Feinberg, PhD, wrote a book titled *Corporate Bigamy*. In his book, he tells of interviewing one hundred top CEOs in the Fortune 500—an annual list ranking 500 of the largest U.S. corporations by total revenue. Dr. Feinberg asked the question, "What is necessary to go to the top in your career and stay there?" And the consensus was this: you build a successful career on honesty and character and integrity and motivation. They summed it up by saying anybody dishonest who thinks they can go to the top and stay there is dumb. That's about as strong as you can get.

And yet more than 70 percent of all of the businessmen on television—they aren't as hard on the women—are depicted as con artists and/or crooks, the exact opposite of the reality of life.

STEP 4: VOCABULARY

If you want to reach your goals, you need to change your vocabulary from negative to positive. Remember when that opportunity clock would sound off every morning at 5:30 and I would get up and jog? A lot of people have asked me, "During that time did you really enjoy getting up and doing all of that running?" I'm going to tell you, I absolutely hated it.

I'd reach over and turn off that clock and lay there for a few moments thinking to myself, *Ziglar, what's a forty-six-year-old fat boy like you doing getting up and running all over the neighborhood?* Then I'd look down at my forty-one-inch waistline and think, *Do you really want to look like you, or do you want to look like the guy in the jockey shorts?* Well, I didn't want to look like me, so I would crawl out of bed feeling like a martyr. I'd put on that fancy running outfit, head for the front door, and out I'd go to start jogging. But I was grumbling all the way, *What am I doing? Trying to kill myself? But I said I was going to do it...so I'm gonna do it.*

If you want to reach your goals, you need to change your vocabulary from negative to positive.

Oh, and don't think for a minute that I didn't tell people all over the country about the sacrifice I was making. How I would get up in the morning and do this thing because I was committed to do it—and if I'm committed to do it, I'm going to do it. If I said it once, I said it a thousand times. I would raise my voice and say, "You gotta paaaay the price!" What a bunch of baloney.

Reality hit me on a beautiful spring day in Portland, Oregon, with the temperature about 78 degrees as I was running on the Portland State

University campus. All of a sudden I became aware of the fact that I was breathing easily and the ground was flowing smoothly beneath my feet.

And that day, friend, for the first time I understood you don't *pay* the price for good health, you *enjoy the benefits of good health.* You don't *pay* the price for success, you pay the price for failure—you *enjoy the benefits of success.* You don't *pay* the price for a good marriage, you pay the price for a poor one—you *enjoy the benefits of a good marriage.*

If you really want to reach your goals, you need to change your vocabulary from negative to positive. You really do.

> ✓ You don't **pay** the price for good health, you **enjoy the benefits of good health.** You don't **pay** the price for success, you pay the price for failure—you **enjoy the benefits of success.**

STEP 5: SMALL BITES

If you want to reach your goal, divide the journey into small bites. When I was writing the book and losing the weight, the doctor told me to lose thirty-seven pounds, but he didn't tell me how long to take to do it. I was writing the book at that point, and I figured, based on what I had already done, that it would take me ten months to write the book. So I thought, *Well, if it's going to take me ten months to write the book, I'll just lose the weight as I'm writing. I'll break it down and will lose three and seven tenths pounds a month.* Remember, you have to be able to see yourself as already there. You have to emotionally commit yourself to it—to visualize and believe that you can get there.

I knew that I could lose three and seven tenths pounds a month. That's not even a pound a week. So, I was totally, completely, 100 percent confident that I could do it. I was so confident that I didn't even bother to get started for twenty-nine days.

Do you know anyone who's a "half-a-minder" and "gonna-doer"? They are the ones who are gonna do this and they have half a mind to do that. Those people invariably end up being the never-doers. They always have excuses such as the kids keep me too busy, it's the holiday season, it's football season, the weather is too bad or too good, the family needs my time, it's summer vacation time, etc.

Friend, if you have to wait for your aunt to move out or your spouse to get on the day shift, or you're waiting for the primaries to end, the new senator to be elected, the interest rate to drop or inflation to slow down, the new advertising campaign to get started, the new model to come out—if you are the one waiting on change "out there" before making any decisions internally or taking any actions, you are wasting valuable time. Start right now.

After wasting those twenty-nine days, I discovered that if I lost one inch and nine tenths ounces a day, ten months later to the ounce and to the day, I would lose the weight. And that is exactly what happened. Exactly.

> If you are the one waiting on change "out there" before making any decisions internally or taking any actions, you are wasting valuable time. Start right now.

Back to my book. *See You at the Top* is 384 pages; and counting foreign editions, it has sold more than two million copies, as mentioned previously. I wrote one and one fourth pages a day every day for ten months. I took small bites out of it every day.

How do you build a magnificent marriage? It's not the great honeymoon, big Christmas, or expensive vacation, it's the everyday acts of time, respect, affection, and courtesy that you show to each other. You raise positive kids in a negative world with daily injections of love and direction and concern. You build a magnificent career, regardless of the field, by doing the little things that count and make a positive difference. It's about taking small bites that will determine whether you reach your goal or not.

Let me stress that what I'm really talking about is simply going in a definite direction and organizing your time. I'm suggesting that by following these procedures, you will be taking control. It's been said that 90 percent of all independent people, particularly in the world of sales and entrepreneurial organizations and medicine and law and so many other careers, are dictated to and subjected to the whims of just about everybody who comes and goes imposing on their time, giving them things to do. They don't know how to get out from under these wasters of their time. When we have direction in our lives, we are in control of our lives. You need to *become a time miser.*

STEP 6: SHAPE UP

If you want to reach your goals, you need to shape up. There've been numerous studies that confirm there is a definite correlation among the most successful people in the United States between the physical and mental and the spiritual, and people who take care of themselves physically.

A close friend of mine, Dr. Forest Tennant, has been the number-one drug authority in this country. When Howard Hughes and Elvis Presley died, they sent the autopsies to Dr. Tennant. He has the largest research staff, is a consultant for the NFL, NASCAR, the Los Angeles Dodgers, the Justice Department, etc. Dr. Tennant deals at the very top of the corporate ladder.

He says that CEOs almost never smoke cigarettes, drink booze, or get involved in drugs. Not only that, but one study revealed that their interests in the spiritual aspects of life are considerably higher than in the general population as well. In addition to that, these successful people are committed to what they're doing, so they don't have time for foolishness and would rather spend time with their families.

We need to shape up physically, shape up mentally, and shape up spiritually—all are so closely tied together. I'm somewhat of a fanatic about physical conditioning because it has made such a dramatic difference in my life. My energy level is so much higher; I can do things today at age sixty-one that I could not do when I was twenty-five. What I am saying is that inside of you there is incredible potential—physically, mentally, and spiritually.

It isn't easy, but when you're tough on yourself, life is going to be infinitely easier on you.

STEP 7: HANDLING DISAPPOINTMENT

If you really want to reach your goals, you have to know how to respond to disappointment. In the fall of 1987, the University of Notre Dame was playing Penn State University. They were in the fourth quarter and Penn State was ahead. Notre Dame was driving toward the end zone. I admired Penn State's Coach Paterno enormously, but Lou Holtz is my buddy.

It's not what happens to us, it's how we handle what happens to us that makes the difference.

I was really pulling for Notre Dame and they drove all the way down the field. There was about a minute left in the game. The tight end from Notre Dame broke completely free into the end zone. The quarterback hit him with a pass. I mean he hit him right in the hands. He catches it and Notre Dame wins. He drops it, Penn State wins. He dropped the ball. Ten of the eleven players on the Notre Dame team did everything they were supposed to do. One of them dropped the ball.

It will be very interesting to see what happens in life to the young man who dropped the ball and to the quarterback. Knowing Lou Holtz as I do, as wise as he is, as much compassion as he has and his skill in human relations and his natural fairness, I have an idea that long ago he had enabled the young man to put it behind him.

I tell this story primarily for this reason. There are going to be those occasions in life when you do everything that you're supposed to do—and somebody else is going to drop the ball. That's part of life. But *it's not what happens to us, it's how we handle what happens to us that makes the difference.*

Motivation follows action.

STEP 8: DISCIPLINE

If you want to reach your goals, you *must discipline yourself.* One of the toughest things you will ever do is what I'm now going to suggest. When you arise in the morning, you need to take your goal planner or your performance plan or whatever it is that you're using and put it under your pillow. That night when you get ready to lie down, you can't go to sleep until you have spent ten minutes recording your activities of the day and planning the six things you're going to work on tomorrow. You need to discipline yourself to do that.

A lot of people say, "I'll do it when I'm motivated to do it." But *motivation follows action.* Motivation, incidentally, also creates energy. Dr. Tennant says that when you jog, you activate the pituitary gland. Then the pituitary gland floods the system with endorphins, and that can be one of the most exciting events in your day. Discipline yourself to get in shape in all aspects of your life.

STEP 9: DIRECTION

I touched a little bit earlier on this subject. What do you do when obstacles arise? Change your direction to reach your objective—but don't change your decision to get there.

STEP 10: SHARING YOUR GOALS

You need to share certain goals and not share other goals. Over the years I've been asked one question more than almost any other, "Who should I share my goals with?"

There is one basic rule that is not set in concrete, but I believe it's very valid: share your "go-up" goals very, very carefully. If you want to be the starting quarterback, the number-one salesperson, an author, a music composer—share it only with those individuals whom you have every reason to believe will encourage you in those goals.

For example, if two salespeople, John and Paula, represent the same company and the same product, and John tells Paula, "I'm going to be number one this year! I'm going to sell more than anybody!" Well, Paula isn't going to support him in that goal because she wants to be number one too. But if John shares his goal with the sales manager, the manager will give him the kind of encouragement that John really needs. Be very careful with whom you share your go-up goals. Share them only with people who will give you the encouragement you need.

On the other hand, you can share your "give-up" goals with everybody. Give-up goals are things you want to give up like smoking, drinking, overeating, losing your temper, being rude, etc. If it is a give-up goal, it has to do with self-improvement. Put yourself on the spot and ask for help. Having others help you track your give-up goals can be beneficial—as can being a team player.

Be very careful with whom you share your go-up goals. Share them only with people who will give you the encouragement you need.

STEP 11: TEAM PLAYER

To reach your goals, you need to become a team player. Have you ever seen a flock of Canadian geese flying overhead? If you watch carefully, you'll notice three things. First, they fly in a V formation. Second, one leg of that V is longer than the other. And third, from time to time there appears to be some confusion in the flock.

Have you noticed those things? Have you ever wondered why one leg of that V is always longer than the other one? Obviously, it has more geese in it. The reason they fly in a V formation, though, is because in wind tunnel tests, the V formation permits the geese to fly about 70 percent farther than they otherwise could fly. And the reason for the confusion is because the lead goose grows tired of fighting that headwind. Consequently, periodically the leader rests, which causes the apparent confusion. They work together to get to where they want to go—it's a team effort.

Previously, I mentioned Joe Paterno, Penn State football coach. When he was coach, his was one of the most team-oriented teams in the country. If you're a football fan, you've probably noticed that the Penn State uniforms are not the classiest among the collegiate ranks. As a matter of fact, you might put them fairly close to the bottom. Joe Paterno is one of the few coaches who does not put the names of his players on the jerseys. They strictly go by numbers. They don't look for the outstanding star, they look for outstanding players—within the team concept. In 1988 when Penn State played for the 1987 championship against the University of Miami, they played against Vinny Testaverde, the Heisman Trophy winner reputed to be the finest collegiate player in, back then, the past five to ten years.

But Penn State, the team, beat Testaverde and his team. When Penn State, the team, played against Herschel Walker and the University of Georgia, Penn State, the team, beat Herschel and the University of Georgia. They win as a team. You might ask, "What happens to the individuals? Do they sacrifice their careers in order to become team players?" The answer is no. Penn State University had the third largest number of active players in the National Football League of any college in America during the time when Paterno was coach. Now why would that be? The pro scouts and their pro teams prefer the outstanding talent who can function as a member of the team more than they do just the star who is not as team-oriented.

By putting the team first, they end up first. It's still true—you can have everything in life you want if you just help enough other people get what they want.

You reach your goals by becoming a team player. If you're married, ideally when you and your mate get together and go over your plans and work together, the chances of you both individually reaching your goals are enhanced. The January 13, 1986 issue of *U.S. News and World Report* reported on the 1 million millionaires in America at that time. Something intriguing was discovered. For example, considerably less than 1 percent of all of the millionaires in the U.S. earned their money in entertainment, television, music, athletics, and radio all combined. The typical millionaire had been working twenty to thirty years supplying basic human needs in life—and the typical millionaire was still married to their high school or college sweetheart. *Team* is so very important.

The pro scouts and their pro teams prefer the outstanding talent who can function as a member of the team more than they do just the star who is not as team-oriented.

STEP 12: BREAKING BARRIERS

To reach your goals, you have to know how to train fleas. You've probably heard the one about the two fleas at the bottom of the hill and one said, "Well, do we walk or take a dog?" I guess that's a little corny, but it leads to the fact that you can train fleas by putting them in a jar, put the lid on the jar, and those fleas will jump up and hit the lid over and over and over and over. After a while, though, you'll notice that although they continue to jump, they no longer hit the top. That's an absolute fact. Then, you can take the lid off and the fleas will continue to jump but not jump out—they have conditioned themselves to jump just so high. And once they've conditioned themselves to jump just so high, that's all there is—there ain't no more.

Humans are exactly the same way. They start out in life ready to climb the mountain, write the book, and break the record. Along the way they bump their head or stub a toe and they become what we call *sniops* (spelled

SNIOP). Those are people who are *Susceptible to the Negative Influence of Other People.*

A classic example is the four-minute mile. For years athletes have said, "I'm gonna break the barrier! I'm going to run a mile in four minutes or less." They would toe the line and get ready to go. But even as they were toeing the line, they knew they'd never break it because the coach's voice would come back to them, "Man, you'll never make it. You might do it in 4:02, maybe even 4:01, but nobody will ever break the four-minute barrier. Then words of the doctor would come back to them, "A four-minute mile? The human body can't stand it." Nobody broke that barrier until Roger Bannister came along.

First of all, Roger Bannister was a superb athlete. Second, he had a tremendous positive mental attitude. Third, he was a goal setter personified. He measured his strides. He had broken it down to that minute degree. He had timed himself for the quarter mile, a half mile, three-quarter, and so forth. He had himself in peak condition. And, he was a team player. He had three other guys serving as pacers with him.

The plans were set and he ran a mile in a little less than four minutes. One of the classic pictures of all time shows Roger Bannister crossing the line as John Landy of Australia, who had been in the lead, had turned around to see where Bannister was—while Bannister was sweeping by on the other side. A lot of lessons in that event—the difference between winning and being second is very small. Number two, it's not a very good idea to be looking back when you ought to be looking ahead.

Since Bannister broke the barrier, there have been thousands of racers who have run a mile in less than four minutes. The reason? Bannister set the way. When he broke the barrier, he proved that it was not a physical impossibility, it was a psychological barrier that had been broken.

A barrier breaker is someone driven internally—not influenced by the outward negatives of life. That person understands that you can have everything in life you want if you just help enough other people get what they want. Barrier breakers don't tell other people where to get off; they show them how to get on. They don't try to see through people; they see people through.

You can have everything in life you want if you just help enough other people get what they want.

STEP 13: SEE THE FUTURE

To reach your goals, you need to see "the reaching." You need to see yourself as already being there and reaching your objective. As you know, I pasted that fella in the jockey shorts on my bathroom mirror and I saw myself as being that kind of an individual, at that weight. Likewise, you need to see yourself in your new home. You need to see yourself and your spouse enjoying the relationship that you had dreamed of enjoying earlier when you were dating. You need to see your children growing up successfully in your mind to be the kind of adults you want them to be.

The basketball player who is successful literally sees the ball going through the net before he ever turns it loose. Jack Nicklaus said he got in his best practice on the golf course even before he arrived at the golf course. While flying his plane to get there, he mentally played every hole in his mind's eye. He saw the ball splitting the middle of the fairway. He saw the ball landing gently on the green. He saw that putt going into the hole.

Many years ago, a young sailor was at sea on a sailing ship. A squall came up and he was ordered aloft to trim the sails. While up there, he made the mistake of looking down and the turbulence of the sea combined with the roll of the ship caused him to become nauseated and he started to lose his balance. An older sailor underneath shouted to him, "Look up, son, look up!" The young sailor looked up and immediately regained his balance. The message is very clear—when the outlook isn't good, and it often isn't, try the uplook, it's always good.

You need to see the reaching. When you reach any of your goals, you need to immediately set a new one.

I fervently believe that the suggestions in this book will make a dramatic difference in your life. I have not told you to do one single thing that I have not done myself. When I had the dream of becoming a speaker, I visualized in my imagination doing everything you've read. I saw myself on the platform. I saw the audiences sitting there in wild-eyed astonishment that a mere mortal could utter such incredible words of wisdom. In the speeches I made in my mind, when I would tell a joke, the audience wouldn't just laugh, they would roll up and down the aisles. On occasion when I finished, there was a spontaneous ten-minute standing ovation. It was phenomenal. The beautiful thing about the imagination is that you can let it run absolutely wild.

> When the outlook isn't good, and it often isn't, try the uplook, it's always good.

Let me encourage you to be very careful about following the exact directions that I've been giving. Be very careful about seeing the reaching and using your imagination in this way. Be absolutely certain that you really do want to accomplish those objectives—because if you do, it works. I can tell you it works. These principles and steps to take to reach your goals are down to earth—each one is practical on a daily basis. When you take hold of these ideas and follow the procedures, you *will* accomplish your goals.

BETWEEN THE GOALPOSTS

You set your goals at the end of Chapter 2; now after reading Chapter 3, you know the steps to take toward achieving your goals. On a scale from 1 (disinterested) to 10 (very interested) how interested are you in seriously committing to the thirteen attributes required to reach your four goals?

Commitment ________

Accountability ________

Solid Foundation ________

Vocabulary ________

Small Bites ________

Shape Up ________

Handling Disappointment ________

Discipline ________

Direction ________

Sharing Your Goals ________

Team Player ________

Breaking Barriers ________

See the Future ________

BEYOND THE GOALPOSTS

Congratulations for setting your goals! Now you can use the formula to reach your goals!

Tell the Lou Holtz story in your own words, taking to heart the moral of it and the end run.

Zig Ziglar's first three sentences of his best-selling book were powerful. Write three sentences that would begin your book:

Are you as committed to your goal as Zig was about his goal of losing weight and publishing a best-seller? Yes or No. If not, why not?

Are you willing to write your plans for the next day—every evening? How do you rate your time management skills? If not a 10, how can you improve managing your time?

To reach your goals, a solid foundation of honesty, good character traits, integrity, loyalty, trust, love, and faith are vital. Which of these characteristics is your strong point? ____________ Which is your weakest? ____________ What can you do to improve your weakest point?

Can you see the positive in a negative situation? Rather than a "Pollyanna," pie-in-the-sky attitude, goal reachers can always find something good in whatever circumstances they face. Can you?

"You don't pay the price for success, you pay the price for failure—you ***enjoy the benefits*** of success." Write this truth in your own words using a personal experience. For example, "I didn't pay the price for good health, I enjoy the benefits of good health because I exercise regularly and eat healthy foods."

How good are you at visualizing and believing and emotionally committing yourself to your goals?

Very Good   Somewhat Good   No Good

Are you a:

Go-Getter   Half-a-Minder   Gonna-Doer   Never-Doer

Why did you choose this title? What can you do to become a go-getter?

Do you believe the research that says there is a correlation among the most successful people in the United States and their physical, mental, and spiritual health? ________ From 1 to 10, how would you rate your:

Physical health ________

Mental health ________

Spiritual health ________

Are these ratings those of a successful person? ________________

Have you ever dropped the ball during an important project? What was the outcome? Were you berated or forgiven?

Has someone else ever dropped the ball during your important project? Did you berate the person or forgive? What does forgiving reveal about your character?

What does the phrase "motivation follows action" mean to you as an individual?

____

As a career person?

____

As a boss or employee?

____

As a spouse?

____

As a parent?

____

Can you name two or three people with whom you can share your deepest thoughts, ideas, and feelings, knowing they will be encouraging, not critical? If not, try and cultivate such a relationship, as confidants are an important part of life. True? ______________

In addition to the few confidants, a team of positive thinking, speaking, and acting people is also vital for a life full of abundance. Name six to eight of your formal or informal team members:

____________________ ____________________

____________________ ____________________

____________________ ____________________

____________________ ____________________

List the dreams or wild ideas you are reaching for .

Now see yourself with each of those things. If that is hard for you, scour magazines or the Internet to find an image that prompts you to take your dream and ideas to the next level—confirming that each is attainable. Post them where you see them daily.

CHAPTER 4

YOUR DESIRES OF LIFE

A number of years ago, before it was too dangerous to do so, I would occasionally pick up a hitchhiker. One day I picked up a young fellow as I was on my way to Pensacola, Florida for a speaking engagement.

At one time in my life, I felt a moral responsibility to try to enthuse, inspire, motivate, invigorate, and educate every human being I came in touch with. Well, I obviously had a captive audience in this particular instance, because the young man could not do anything but listen to me while in the car. We chatted along the way, then I started espousing my philosophy of life and how wonderful things are. When I finished my little dissertation, I said, "Well, son, how would you like to make a lot of money and be really successful in life?"

I saw a far-away look in his eyes and a wistful expression came across his face, and he said, "Oh, I wouldn't mind."

That's not exactly the reaction of someone with an overwhelming desire for being successful.

Desire enables us to change the hot water of mediocrity to the steam of outstanding success.

MISSION

Most great teachers, brilliant musicians, outstanding athletes, marvelous parents, and effective government leaders have had a tremendous desire to be successful in whatever they are doing. Whether it's to be the best household executive, the best student, or the best banker, it requires a considerable amount of desire in order to get to being the best at anything.

A 1986 Harvard study revealed that outstanding people have one thing in common—an absolute sense of mission. They don't go to work every day—they go on a mission. They have something they really want to do. I believe that *desire* is the great equalizer. If we use enough of it and if we have enough of it, *desire enables us to change the hot water of mediocrity to the steam of outstanding success.* Little things make a big difference.

When you heat water to 211 degrees, you have really hot water. You can take that hot water and make a cup of coffee or tea or you can shave with it. But if you add one more degree, that hot water converts to steam. Now you can take that steam and propel a locomotive literally across the country or you can take a steamship and propel it all the way around the world. It's the additional degree that makes the difference.

Most salespeople will tell you there is absolutely no commission on the sale they *almost* make. And there is not much excitement in *almost* sinking the putt or *almost* getting a hit or *almost* anything. But the difference between doing it and not doing it many times is measured in minute amounts.

When I think about desire, I think of a baseball player who, back in 1946, played for the St. Louis Browns. At the time, the Browns were arguably the weakest major league team to ever take the field. This certain baseball player only lasted one year. He was an outfielder. He was not even a regular. He never hit a home run. And yet I believe that he would qualify as a legitimate candidate for the Hall of Fame. The young man's name was Pete Gray, and as a young man he had a burning desire, an absolutely overwhelming ambition to play major league ball. And he did despite the fact that he had only one arm. But that one arm coupled with a tremendous desire enabled him to get all the way to the major leagues.

So many times, desire is what makes the difference. I have a friend who often says that you take the hand you're dealt and utilize it to the best of your ability; and with that combination, you are going to be successful in many, many fields of endeavor.

ABILITY

Many people complain about not having enough talent to do the job. Have you ever heard someone say, "If I just had that person's talent, I could..." or "If I could sing like her..." or "If I could sell like that guy..." or "If I could handle objections like that person...." What they often are saying is, "If I just had somebody else's ability, I could...." Remember, if you're not using the ability you already have, you won't use somebody else's.

One of the best-known parables is the story of the talents. A man was going to a faraway country, so he called three of his servants together. He gave five talents to one servant, he gave two talents to another servant, and he gave one talent to the last servant. He said, "I'm going away and when I come back, I will expect you to report on what you did with your talents."

When he returned, he called the servant he'd given five talents and said, "Well, how did you do?" The servant said, "I did good. I took those five talents and put them to work, and now I have ten talents."

The man said, "Well done, good and faithful servant. Because you've been faithful with a few, I will give you many." And he gave him more talents. And then he said some exciting words, "Enter into the joy of the Lord."

Then he called the second servant and asked how he did while he was away. The servant said, "I did good. I put my two talents to work and now I have four." The man told him he did good and told him the same thing as he told the first servant.

Then he went to the one who had the one talent and asked how he did. This time he heard a different answer. He heard from one of the crybabies of life—those who always think, *If I just had more, I would've used what I had.* The servant answered the man saying, "I knew that you were a hard and cruel master, that you reaped where you did not sow. And I knew that you were unfair and unjust, and so I took the one talent you gave me and I buried it, and here it is."

The man's response contains some of the harshest words in that portion of the Bible, "You wicked and lazy servant." And he took the one talent away from him and gave it to the one with ten talents. Now understand what I'm going to say next is pure conjecture; I have no reason whatever for believing this, and yet it seems to me that it is consistent with everything I know about life. I believe that if the servant with the one talent had tried to do something with it, even had he lost it I believe he would have been given another chance. I really believe that. But because he didn't use it, it was taken away from him. The law says very clearly that if we use what we have, we will be given more to use.

In a previous chapter in this book you identified a lot of things you thought you wanted. You wrote them all down. Then you identified things that you couldn't work on right now, but I told you not to eliminate those from the list because later, as you grow and mature and develop, they will become legitimate goals in some other area of your life. As you grow, you can do many more things with the talents you have.

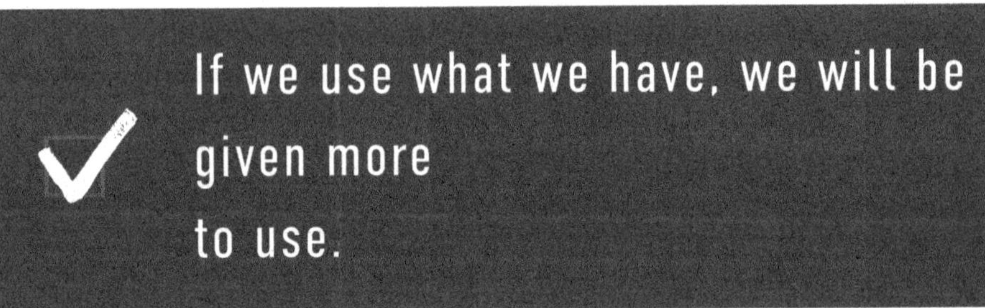

WINNERS AND LOSERS

Knute Rockne, a famous football coach at Notre Dame, said, "I don't like to lose, not so much because it's just a football game, but because the defeat means the failure to reach an objective." I think that's a pretty good way of looking at it. When you use what you have, when you have that desire, the chances of winning are much, much greater.

Rockne pointed out that a lot of people thought they had to be good losers or bad winners. He felt this was a lousy choice. He also pointed out that he had no desire to get enough experience at losing to be a good one. "Show me a good loser," he said, "and I'll show you a loser. Give me eleven *lousy* losers, and I'll give you a national championship football team." He said, "The way a man wins shows much of his character—and the way he loses shows all of it."

However, I'm speaking about the will, determination, and the desire to win. We simply don't have to make the choice between being good losers and bad winners. The more experience we have at winning, the better we can become at being good winners.

"The way a man wins shows much of his character—and the way he loses shows all of it."

DESIRE AND DETERMINATION

When I think of desire, I think of a man named Ben Hogan. I admit I'm a golf fanatic. A lot of people play the game better than I do, but I don't believe there's a human being alive who enjoys the game any more than I do. I just love to get out there and tee that little dude up. So when I start talking about golfers, I talk about Ben Hogan—who might well be the greatest player who ever played the game when you consider everything.

He started his golfing career on a financial shoestring. He literally had almost nothing to eat and stayed in the cheapest places just to survive the tour. Just as he was reaching his peak in the golfing world, one night he and his wife, Valerie, were on their way to another tournament and it was very foggy. Just as he rounded a corner, he saw the oncoming headlights of a Greyhound bus. He instinctively and instantaneously threw himself over in front of his wife to protect her, and that move probably saved both of their lives because the impact shoved the steering wheel all the way back through the driver's seat where he was sitting moments before.

The doctors, and there were many of them, were unanimous in their agreement on one thing—Ben Hogan would be a very, very fortunate man to ever get out of his bed. They all knew he would never be able to walk; and as for ever playing golf again—it was out the question. There was no way. But they simply had not reckoned with the steel will, the tremendous drive, and the outstanding desire that Ben Hogan had. Even as he lay there in the hospital bed, in his head he held those golf clubs in his hands and kept visualizing them. Then he started doing exercises to strengthen his hands.

When he started walking again, with the aid of canes and crutches, he could just barely move around. Eventually, he could stand in his room and hold his putter and then start putting. Later he would go out to the course on crutches and just stand there and swing a club. He would swing and swing and gradually, over months and months, he got stronger and stronger. And, of course, the rest of his story is absolute history. He won tournaments and set records. He did some things that were absolutely impossible. Ben Hogan was not what you might call a natural golfer, but the talent was there. There's no denying he had talent, but there were many golfers who had infinitely more. Yet nobody had any more desire to make it than Ben Hogan did.

Enthusiasm sometimes has to be tempered with direction.

TEMPERED ENTHUSIASM

Enthusiasm sometimes has to be tempered with direction. I try to remember that because sometimes people get the impression that all they have to do is have the desire and then they can do just about anything—and oftentimes that is not quite the case.

In the 1988 Olympics in Calgary, Canada, anyone with any interest in sports remembers a young man named Dan Jansen who was the U.S. speed skater favored to win a gold medal. Surely 90 percent of the people in the world, with the exception of those who were competing directly with him, were pulling for Dan Jansen—as that very morning his older sister had died of leukemia. His desire to win that gold medal was absolutely overwhelming. He had trained faithfully. He was favored to win.

And yet on the very first turn, as one of those quirks of fate happens, his skates flew out from under him and he crashed into the wall. He was out of the race before it even got started. It had taken him a tremendous amount of desire to get to the Olympics. His desire helped him get where he was.

But his desire *after* that accident would determine what he would do with the rest of his life. How did he handle it? Would that desire be channeled in the right direction? Yes! Dan Jansen went on to win the gold in the last race of his Olympic career—at the 1994 games in Norway.

INTELLIGENT IGNORANCE

Everyone faces some serious disappointments, defeats, and setbacks during their lifetimes. We have to learn how to handle those situations. But desire creates what we call "intelligent ignorance." And if you have a lot of real intelligent ignorance, a lot of things can happen. For example, in the world of sales, brand-new salespeople come in and don't really understand all of the finer techniques of selling. But they are so gung-ho on their product and they are really enthusiastic about it. They believe it's the greatest thing since sliced bread and they believe that for them this represents a tremendous opportunity. They believe everybody alive should have this fantastic product—and the net result is, they go out and sell rings around the old, established pros. This has happened time and time again.

Desire makes a difference in many occasions. Desire manifests itself a lot of times in basketball games and football games when the coach or the referee blows the whistle and a substitute jumps off the bench and in comes a fresh body. Here's a second stringer who wants to really impress the coach and the crowd. He or she thinks, *When I get out there, I'm really going to show the coach a thing or two...and who knows, maybe I'll be starting the next game!* I have seen substitutes on many occasions actually perform better than the starting players. They have that little extra desire that makes a difference.

I believe that the bumblebee is a classic example of what intelligent ignorance is really all about. If you've done any reading and studying about aerodynamics, you know that the bumblebee cannot fly—its body is too heavy and its wings are too light. It is written that it is impossible for it to fly. But the bumblebee doesn't read; the bumblebee flies.

Henry Ford is a classic case of a man who had intelligent ignorance. Although he had a limited education, he made a fortune manufacturing the Model T and then the Model A vehicle. Then one day he had a wild idea—he conceived the building of a V8 engine. Mr. Ford was not an engineer, so he called his high-priced staff together and said, "I want you to build for me a V8 engine."

They tried to humor the old man a little bit; they didn't want to put him down too hard. So they gently explained to him that the V8 was an engineering impossibility. He said, "Well, I understand that, but we have to have one and I want you to build it and I want you to go do it right now." They made a half-hearted effort, spent quite a few dollars, and came back a few months later and said, "Mr. Ford, just like we said, the V8 engine is an impossibility. It can't be done."

He said, "Obviously, you don't understand. We have to have a V8 engine, and you're going to build one. Now go build it!" Well, this time they went and spent a little more money and stayed a little bit longer and finally they came back to him and said, "Mr. Ford, it just can't be done."

This time Henry Ford really hit the ceiling. He blew his stack. He said, "Apparently I'm not communicating my message to you! The V8 engine is *going* to be built and *you're* going to build it for me. Now I want you to go out there and this time don't come back until you tell me the news that you did it. You are in fact *going* to build a V8 engine." They built the V8 engine. One man had the intelligent ignorance that made it happen. Henry Ford said, "I'm looking for a lot of men with an infinite capacity for not knowing what can't be done."

> It is written that it is impossible for it to fly. But the bumblebee doesn't read; the bumblebee flies.

I CAN

Everyone and every company in America needs to think in terms of *I can* rather than *I can't.* We need more people who don't know what can't be done; they are the ones who will go out and do it. I love what Miss Mamie McCullough, our "I can lady," says. She's the one who took the book *See You at the Top* and converted it into a course that is being taught all over the country. She thought of this one day and has had a tremendous amount of fun with it. And the nice thing is, it makes a lot of sense.

The first day she said to the class, "To the very best of your ability, I want you to describe for me an 'I can't.' What does an 'I can't' look like?" And the students wrestled with that question for a moment or two, and then Miss McCullough said, "We don't know what an 'I can't' looks like, do we? Now I would like you to describe for me an 'I can.'" And they described big cans, little cans, round cans, square cans, long cans, short cans, all kind of cans. "In other words, there is no such thing as *can't*—you can't see it, smell it, taste it, feel it, or touch it. But you can smell, feel, taste, touch *can.* So I can't doesn't exist, but I can does. We're going to call this the I can course, and I believe that is the spirit we need more of in this country of ours—the I can spirit."

General Creighton Abrams Jr. took intelligent ignorance to another level. In World War II, General Abrams, during the Battle of the Bulge, was completely surrounded by enemy forces—they were to the north, south, east, and west. His staff officers came to him in a panic and told him they were completely surrounded. In essence, he responded, "Well, that's magnificent; let's let the troops know that for the first time in the history of this entire campaign we can now attack the enemy in any direction we choose."

It's not what the situation is, it's what we make of the situation we are in. We just need to remember that the darkest night since the beginning of time did not darken all the stars—that even on the brightest day, you can still go down into a well and can look up and see the stars from that dark spot. Sometimes when things look the very darkest is when we can see the gleam of light that will lead us to where we really want to go. But we have to have that *desire* in order to do that.

It's not what the situation is, it's what we make of the situation we are in.

BETWEEN THE GOALPOSTS

"Outstanding people have one thing in common—an absolute sense of mission. They don't go to work every day—they go on a mission. They have something they really want to do. I believe that desire is the great equalizer." How deeply do these statements affect you? Write about the goal or goals that would make you change your attitude from going to work to going on a mission.

How effective are you at using your talents and abilities? Do you maximize skills by practicing them, utilizing them at every opportunity? What can you do to improve or enhance your talents and abilities to help you reach your goals?

What did you learn from reading about Ben Hogan and Dan Jansen? Did their stories encourage you or discourage you? Why?

Would your life move forward quicker if you had more "intelligent ignorance"?

It's not what the situation is, it's what you make of the situation you are in. Cite a few "situations" you are in right now and then write what you are going to make of those situations.

BEYOND THE GOALPOSTS

Outstanding people have an absolute sense of ***mission.*** Define what your life's "mission" means to you:

Because "desire enables you to change the hot water of mediocrity to the steam of outstanding success," what areas in your life do you identify as mediocre?

What is the first area you will change from mediocre to outstandingly successful?

In what area(s) have you "run out of steam" and need to heat up?

Do you agree with Zig's conclusion that the third servant would have received a second chance if he had ***done something, anything*** with the talent he was given rather than burying it? ________ Have you kept a "talent"—skill or knowledge—buried when it should have been multiplied to help yourself and others? Yes or No. Write about that talent(s) and how deep you will dig to resurrect it today:

Rewrite Knute Rockne's quote—"I don't like to lose, not so much because it's just a football game, but because the defeat means the failure to reach an objective"—in your own words, making it personal:

Sit quietly in your favorite spot and think about what you're good at. Perhaps deep down you know you are a good ____________________. In your heart you know you're a good, even a great ____________________. It doesn't have to be a career like a good writer, chef, or nurse. You may be an excellent listener, friend, parent, etc. How can you use this type of "talent" to advance toward your goals, while helping others at the same time? Write your thoughts:

____

____

____

____

Would you rather be a good loser or a bad winner? ____________________ Do you think those are the only two choices in life? Yes or No. Explain your answer.

____

____

____

____

Do you know people who need to temper their enthusiasm? What advice would you give them?

____

____

____

____

Everyone faces disappointments, defeats, and setbacks. How do you usually handle situations that don't turn out as you expected?

With a Smile | Roll with the Punches | Accept and Move On

Kick a Tire | Want Revenge | Give Up

How would you define someone who is intelligently ignorant? Is that you?

____

____

____

____

Name five "I can'ts" and then think about ways that you "can." Put those ways into action.

1. ______________ Action plan: ______________
2. ______________ Action plan: ______________
3. ______________ Action plan: ______________
4. ______________ Action plan: ______________
5. ______________ Action plan: ______________

Do you know any "crybabies of life" who always want more but don't use what they already have? If you could, what would you tell them about that attitude:

A basic life principle is that ***if you use what you have, you will be given more.*** Are you using all of the talents, skills, knowledge, and God-given gifts that you have right now?

If no, why not:

Many people focus more on the situation than the solution. Think about a time when a colleague, spouse, child, or friend was overwhelmed with a problem, but in an effort to console you came up with a solution. Write about how you can do that for yourself when facing a challenge that seems overwhelming.

CHAPTER 5

A LEMON PLUS DESIRE

IF you take a lemon and add desire to it, that's when you get lemonade. I'm sure you've heard that saying before, but it's true. And some of these true stories and illustrations are from years ago, but the principles are as valid today and tomorrow as they were yesterday. Tried and true.

Years and years ago there were cranks on the front of automobiles to start the engine. People had to stand there and turn that sucker as hard as possible to get the engine started. American engineer and inventor Charles Kettering had a lemon. One day he was out there cranking his car and the car lurched forward and broke his arm. Although he was in pain, while holding his broken arm, he thought, *As long as we have this problem, the automobile never will be very popular.* It was his broken arm that led him to invent the electrical self starter motor for automobiles. His lemon was a broken arm. His lemonade was the self-starter.

Jacob Schick had a lemon problem. While prospecting for gold in Alaska, he wanted a shave. But at 40 degrees below zero, shortly after he poured the water in the pan it was frozen. So he invented the electric razor.

Neal Jeffrey was a third-string freshman quarterback at Baylor University and he went to Coach Grant Teaff one day and said, "I want to be the starting quarterback." The problem was, Neal stuttered, and playing quarterback is a position that requires very fluid speech. There's a play clock running and there are only so many seconds to run the plays. But Neal Jeffrey was an unusual young man. Not only did he become the starting quarterback, he led Baylor to its first conference championship in over fifty years, and he was the most valuable player in the Southwest Conference that year, leading his team into the Cotton Bowl.

A lot of times when things happen to us, we can capitalize on them—if we have the right attitude and desire.

TAKE ADVANTAGE OF ADVERSITY

A lot of times when things happen to us, we can capitalize on them—if we have the right attitude and desire.

In Enterprise, Alabama, there is an unusual statue in the town square. It's a statue of a boll weevil. Why did they erect the boll weevil statue? At one time in that part of the country, cotton was the only crop they raised. The economy rose and fell on cotton, and many times people suffered as a direct result. There was no diversification. One particular year the boll weevil ran wild in that area—that destructive bug took a bite out of every cotton plant within forty miles of Enterprise, Alabama. The farmers suffered a total and complete loss. As a result, they recognized at long last what they had been told for many years—they needed to diversify. So they started raising peanuts, soybeans, corn, and many other crops. The economy was so much better that they thought it would be appropriate to erect the statue right there in the center of town because the boll weevil had forced the issue.

If we take a good look at our circumstances, many times we can determine that even the worst of events can be the best thing that has ever happened to us after all.

Charles Goodyear's lemon, for example, was a prison sentence. He was sent to prison because he wouldn't pay a certain bill. While he was there, he had the time and privacy to work on and perfect his process for vulcanizing rubber.

Martin Luther, while he was confined to Waterbury Castle, gave us the German translation of the Bible. John Bunyan wrote the best-selling book *Pilgrim's Progress* when he was in prison. Gene Tunney became the heavyweight boxing champion of the world because he broke both of his hands. Now that might sound like a very unusual statement, but when Tunney was a young fighter, he was fighting with the American Expeditionary Forces during World War II in France. He broke his right hand and then later he broke his left hand. His trainer and the doctors told him that he simply would never become the heavyweight champion of the world because his hands were too brittle—they wouldn't stand up under all the heavy punching that's required.

> If you have enough desire, it certainly will make a difference. No matter the situation, if we add enough desire to it, we can succeed. ✓

But Gene Tunney had a tremendous desire to become the heavyweight champion. He said he would become the most scientific boxer to ever get in the ring. Well, he did win the heavyweight boxing championship from Jack Dempsey, and he did retire as the undefeated heavyweight champion of the world. But ring experts were virtually unanimous in agreement when they said that had he not broken his hands he never would have been the heavyweight champion. Tunney would have undoubtedly attempted to slug it out with Dempsey and would not have learned the boxing skills he needed to win. The smart money of that day said that no man alive could stand up to Jack Dempsey in a toe-to-toe slugging battle. Tunney won the championship because he had the desire, because he broke his hands, and because he took that lemon and made lemonade.

I'm trying to deliver the same message in a hundred different ways so you can understand that when adversity strikes, maybe that adversity is what you need in order to become successful. If you have enough desire, it certainly will make a difference. No matter the situation, if we add enough desire to it, we can succeed.

A STORY TO REMEMBER

I use a lot of examples and illustrations to cover certain points. People tend to remember stories and examples. And if you remember the story or the example, then it's easier to extract the lesson—lessons to inspire and motivate you to keep reaching for your goals.

This particular story is one that I have been telling for twenty-three years, and I tell this story because it involves virtually every principle in which I believe. It covers each one. I was in Kansas City addressing my first really major seminar. After the seminar that day I headed back to my room expecting to have a lonely dinner. But as I stepped off the elevator, the booming voice of a man I've come to know and love as a brother sounded out, "ZIG! Where're you going?" I said, "I'm going to dinner." He said, "Wait a minute, I'll go with you."

When we sat down and started talking, Bernie Lofchick and I became instant friends. Not just buddies, but really close friends. We had about the same size families. His dad and my dad had died when we were very young. We both had gone to work very early in life. He got into the cookware business; I did too at one point. Our commonalities were amazing.

I said, "Bernie, you've certainly come a long way to attend a sales meeting." He said, "Yes, and it really was magnificent. I got some wonderful ideas. It was a great experience." I pressed him a bit more, maybe wanting to hear something negative that I could improve on the next time. So I said,

"Yeah, but it sure cost you a lot of money to come from Winnipeg, Canada to Kansas City for a couple of days."

"Well," he said, "thanks to my son, David, I don't really have to worry about money."

I said, "Bernie, that sounds like a story. Would you share it with me?"

He said, "Sure I will. When our son, David, was born, our joy literally knew no bounds. We were elated. We already had our two girls. Now we had the boy. That's the family we wanted when we got married. But in a few days, we realized something was wrong. David's head hung too limply on the right side of his body. And he drooled too much to be a normal, healthy baby. But the doctor said don't worry about it. He'll grow out of it. But you know, Zig, when it's your baby, you worry about it.

"After about six months, we took him to a specialist who incredibly diagnosed him with a condition he identified as the reverse of club feet, and treated him for that for several weeks. Zig, we knew it was more serious than that. So we went to another specialist and after a very exhaustive examination, he told us that our little boy had cerebral palsy—that he was never going be able to walk or talk or count to ten. The specialist suggested that we put him in an institution for his own good and for the good of the, quote, 'normal members' of the family.

"But Zig, I'm not a buyer I'm a seller. I could not conceive of my son living the life of a vegetable and growing up to be absolutely nothing. I saw him in a different light altogether. So I asked the doctor if he knew of any other doctors. Well, this specialist got highly indignant. He stood up and said, 'I've given you the best advice you'll ever get. I suggest that you take it.'"

Bernie didn't take that advice. He went to another specialist who told him the same thing and then another and another and another. Thirty different specialists said there was no hope for their little boy. Then they heard of Dr. Pearlstein from Chicago, Illinois. Dr. Pearlstein was reputedly the number-one authority in the world on cerebral palsy, but he was so busy that he was booked for two full years in advance.

Bernie finally got the doctor's home phone and called him. He made an arrangement with the doctor so that if there was a cancellation, David would be the first alternate. Just eleven days later, a little boy from Australia canceled, so they bundled up the baby and flew him to Chicago for the examination. It was probably the most comprehensive physical that any child had been given up until that point. They spent hour after hour after hour going over the baby. They threw out all the other findings, all the other x-rays, and started from ground zero for this examination.

They called in the best expert in the world to read the x-rays to tell them what was there—not to make a diagnosis or recommendation, just to tell them what the x-ray revealed. When it was all over, Dr. Pearlstein and his nurses sat down with David's parents. Dr. Pearlstein said, "This little boy has cerebral palsy. He's never going be able to walk or talk or count to ten—if you listen to the prophets of doom. But," he said, "I happen to be solution-conscious not problem-conscious. I believe there is something you can do for this little boy, if you are willing to do your part." David's parents said that they would do anything humanly possible to help their son.

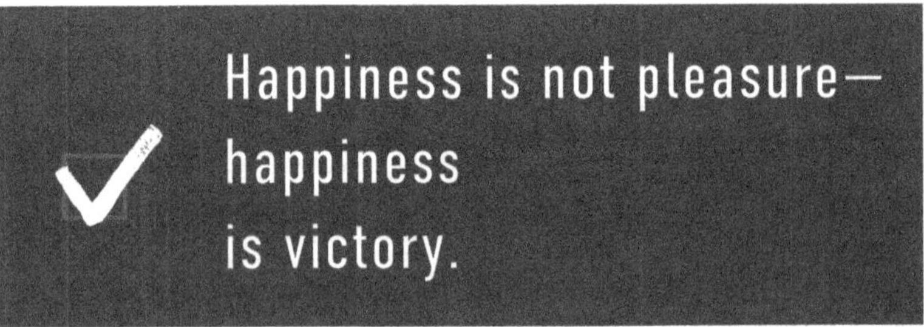

WHATEVER IT TAKES

Now at that time they could not easily afford a very heavy financial burden, but they told the doctor to spell it out and they would do what was necessary. In minute detail he said, "You're going to have to work this little boy beyond all human endurance. Then you're going to have to work him some more. You will have to push him until he literally falls and then you're going to have to pick him up and you'll have to push him some more. You're going to have to be patience personified because there will be many, many months when you will be unable to detect any progress at all. But if you ever stop, he will go all the way back and then you will have to start all over. You have to understand this is a lifetime commitment you're making—not something you do this year, next year, five years, or whatever...this is from now on."

Bernie and Elaine and David went home. They hired a physical fitness expert and a bodybuilder. They built a little gymnasium in the basement of their home and then went to work. It took a number of months before David could even move the length of his own body. One day about two to three years later, Bernie received a call at work from the therapist who said, "I believe David is ready. Come on home." Bernie rushed home. David was down in the gymnasium on a mat getting ready to do a push-up.

As his little body started to rise into the air, the physical and emotional exertion was so great. There was not a dry edge of skin on David's body and the mat looked as if water had been sprinkled on it. When that one perfect push-up was complete, Mom and Dad, his two sisters, David, the therapist, and several of the neighbors who were there broke down in tears, which clearly showed that happiness is not pleasure—happiness is victory.

This story is even more remarkable when we learned that one of America's leading universities had also examined David very carefully and discovered that there were no motor connections to the right side of his body. They said he had no sense of balance; he would never be able to swim or skate or ride a bicycle.

It's one thing to agree with a doctor that you're going to be in it for the next fifteen years—it's another thing to follow through for the next fifteen years.

On October 23, 1971, my wife and I were in Winnipeg, Canada to see David at his bar mitzvah. I wish you could have been there. I wish the television cameras of the world could have been there to see what we saw. That young boy, thirteen years old—whom the doctors said would never be able to walk or talk or count to ten—at that point in his life he had already done as many as 1,100 push-ups in a single day and had run six miles nonstop. He was doing extremely well academically—even doing ninth grade math as a seventh grader at St. John's-Ravenscourt School.

David was running the wheels off his third bicycle, was skating on the neighborhood hockey team, and was one of the best table tennis players in the city of Winnipeg. The next year, to the best of my knowledge, he became the first, and so far as we know, the only victim of cerebral palsy to qualify for an unrated ordinary $100,000 life insurance policy.

PRINCIPLES OF LIFE

The reason I share with you so many of the details of David's story is because it involves the principles that we've been talking about all the way through this book. First of all, there was a *solid foundation.* The doctor was absolutely *honest* with David's parents and in turn they were *honest* with David. As Cavett Roberts said, "*Character* is the ability to carry out a good resolution long after the excitement of the moment has passed." It's one thing to agree with a doctor that you're going to be in it for the next fifteen years—it's another thing to follow through for the next fifteen years.

Integrity—no question of the integrity of all involved from day one. *Loyalty* like you've never seen in a family that became one force. *Trust* was incredible for that family. They were told that there would be years and years when they wouldn't see any change in David's condition—that involved an incredible amount of trust in the outcome. And *love*—one of the most beautiful love stories I've ever heard is this one. When David was about two years of age, at that time they had to start putting heavy leg braces on his legs every evening, and they had to make them progressively tighter.

Every evening when Bernie or his wife would put those leg braces on David, there would be tears in his eyes. He was a beautiful child with green eyes, coal-black hair, and olive complexion. With tears in his eyes, he'd say, "Mommy, do we have to put them on tonight? Daddy, do you have to make them so tight?" Don't you know that any parent in existence would want to give in. But David's parents loved him so much that they said no to the tears of the moment—so they could say yes to the laughter of a lifetime.

When you really love someone, you do what is best for that person. The right, positive *attitude* was exhibited every day and night. Every night Bernie would hold David in his arms and say, "Son, you're a champ. You can do anything you want to do soon. Dad really loves you and Mom really loves you too."

Bernie was one of the first people to get a cassette recorder. Every day, when David was old enough, during his therapy sessions, he would listen to motivation stories that built up his *self-image. Relationships*—probably nobody has ever worked as closely with and in better cooperation with others than David.

David worked all of his life on his *goals.* We talked about daily, long-range, and big goals—David, on many occasions, worked on hourly goals.

When talking about *desire,* this youngster surpassed more than just about anybody I've ever known. The physical effort was absolutely astronomical. David, for one solid year, set his opportunity clock one hour earlier than any other member of the family. When that clock would sound, he'd get up and put on his skates and go out to that frozen swimming pool and practice. It took him one solid winter just to learn how to stand up on the ice. Later, he skated on the neighborhood hockey team.

You've read it many times throughout this book, that you can have everything in life you want if you just help enough other people get what they want. Well, an interesting phenomenon of this story is that while Bernie, in the process of providing David his opportunity in life, not only had to work smarter, he also had to work harder. For seven years, Bernie worked seven days and seven nights every week. He took off only one Friday night in seven years in order to provide the financial necessities for giving his son everything he needed. Bernie Lofchick became an extraordinarily wealthy man. But it goes beyond that.

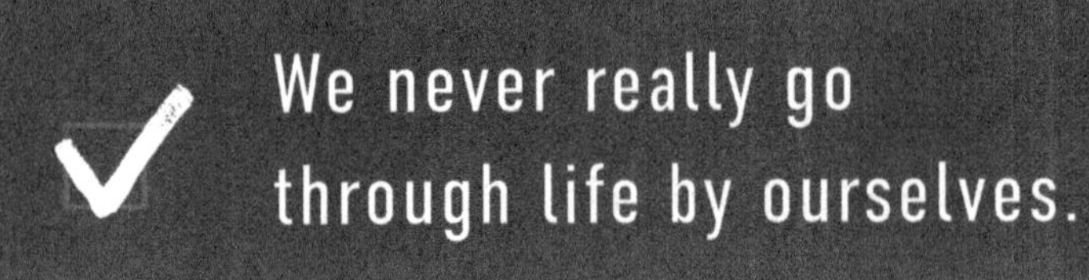

TOUCHING OTHERS

What happens to us affects other people. Let me share another little interesting sideline story about the fact that we never really go through life by ourselves.

I was speaking in Lubbock, Texas, and I told David's story. There was a young couple seated in the very front, and as I told the story, they were visibly moved and asked to visit me privately after the presentation. They asked me the name of the doctor who had taken Dr. Pearlstein's place when he retired. This couple had a little girl, eighteen months old, who was diagnosed with cerebral palsy.

I gave them the doctor's name and they flew her to Chicago for an examination. The doctor examined this little girl thoroughly and when he finished, he said, "This little girl does not have cerebral palsy, she was born prematurely and is a little slow developing. She's been misdiagnosed; but because you have been treating her as if she had cerebral palsy, she has acquired some of the symptoms of the disease. Take her home and treat her as a normal, healthy little girl, and she will be a normal, healthy little girl."

David's story involves a lot of life's most basic principles. It wasn't easy, but I think you'll agree that it's a story that we can learn from in many ways.

Many times over the years I have thought to myself, *I wonder how much bigger and faster and stronger and smarter...how much more David would have been had he been given the same chance in life that you and I were given.*

One day it hit me like a ton of bricks. Had he been given more, he undoubtedly would have ended up with less, maybe a whole lot less. Maybe that's the reason God tells us in His book to thank Him for everything.

What's the end of the story? Well, the story is still being written, but I can bring you up-to-date as of this writing. David Lofchick is a handsome young man, 29 years of age, 195 pounds, healthy and happily married and a proud papa. And for the past two years he's been the number-one condominium salesman in the number-one real estate firm in Winnipeg, Canada. He's having a marvelous time and a marvelous career. The principles he learned as a child are standing him in good stead now and will for the rest of his life.

You see it's not the story I'm really talking about; it's the principles of life. When you apply these principles, take these steps, and follow through, you will accomplish your goals.

BETWEEN THE GOALPOSTS

When "bad" things happen, do you capitalize on them with the right attitude and desire? Or do you more often allow them to immobilize you with doubt and self-deprecation? Write your answers.

____

____

____

____

____

____

____

David's story epitomizes many very important life principles including the following. Have you developed these principles over the course of your life, or are you still working on making them basic fundamentals of your personality, attitude, and your very being? Seriously consider each and then identify each attribute with the corresponding letter: WD=Well-Developed; D=Developed; M=Mediocre; NTBD=Needs to Be Developed; DNH=Desperately Needs Help

Honesty _______

Character _______

Integrity _______

Loyalty _______

Optimistic attitude _______

Trust myself and others _______

Love of self and others _______

Positive self-image _______

Healthy relationships _______

Desire to reach my goals _______

Solid foundation based on all the above _______

Determine to change any NTBD and DNHs to WDs as soon as possible. Write the steps you will take to make those changes happen.

BEYOND THE GOALPOSTS

Reading the lemon/lemonade stories, which one made the most impression on you? Charles Kettering, Jacob Schick, Neal Jeffrey, Charles Goodyear, Martin Luther, John Bunyan, Gene Tunney/Jack Dempsey, or the boll weevil story?

Why is that your choice?

In what ways did the story of David Lofchick affect you and how you look at life?

From David's story, what was your take-away about:

A Solid Foundation

Honesty

Character

Integrity

Loyalty

Trust

Love

Attitude

Self-Image

Relationships

Goals

Desire

How seriously are you applying these principles in your life today?

Write what the following phrase means to you: "Happiness is not pleasure—happiness is victory!"

Without explanation to anyone, if you were to move to another country today, how many people's lives would be impacted? Estimate a number and write it here ________

Now take 2-3 minutes and write the names of anyone whose lives would be affected by your absence:

Count the names and compare with the number you wrote. If you would take an hour to write the names, the list still wouldn't include all the people you have impacted over your lifetime. How does that fact affect you? Do you realize how important you are to so many people beyond your immediate family? Does knowing this impact your current and/or future goals? Write your thoughts:

CHAPTER 6

NO FREE LUNCH

MANY years ago a wise old king called all of his wise men together and said, "I want you to go out and compile for me all the wisdom of the ages. I want you to put it in book form so we can leave it for posterity." So, they went out and worked a long time. They came back and had twelve huge volumes.

The wise old king looked at them and said, "Well, I'm confident that is the wisdom of the ages, but that's too lengthy; people won't read all of that. Condense it." They went out and came back this time with one huge volume.

Again the wise old king said it is still too long, condense it. Then they came back with just a chapter, then a page, then a paragraph, and finally with a sentence.

The king looked at the sentence and said, "That's it! That is truly the wisdom of the ages. As soon as everyone everywhere learns this, we will have solved many of our problems."

Work is the foundation of all business, the source of all prosperity, and the parent of genius.

The sentence simply said, "There ain't no free lunch."

Now the wise old king literally hit the nail on the head. When people learn that if they want to occupy their places in the sun, they have to expect some blisters, then much will have been accomplished. Work is the price we pay to travel the highway of success. We can best guard against losing our shirts by keeping our sleeves rolled up. Many people believe success is dependent upon the glands; and, of course, they're right if they're talking about sweat glands.

The United States of America was built by people who worked and pulled on the oars, not by those who rested on the oars. Read that sentence again and think about it—it's important. Somebody wrote that *work is the foundation of all business, the source of all prosperity, and the parent of genius.* Work can do more to advance youth than his or her own parents. Work is represented in the humblest savings and has laid the foundation of every fortune. Work is the salt that gives life its savor; but it must be loved before it can bestow its greatest blessings and achieve its greatest ends. *When loved, work makes life sweet, purposeful, and fruitful.*

When loved, work makes life sweet, purposeful, and fruitful.

WORK AND INTEGRITY

Since the beginning of time everyone agrees that you can't get something for nothing. People in government, education, religion, industry, every area of life agree there's no free lunch. But then for no good reason, some states decided to legalize horse racing, dog racing, casinos, state lotteries, and such. No wonder our kids are confused. One minute we're saying you have to work, and the next minute we're saying let's gamble our way to prosperity.

A wise man observed that the "success family" has work as the father and integrity as the mother. You may be thinking, *Now wait a minute Ziglar, through these pages you've told me that I have to have a good, solid foundation and I agree with that. And I have to have goals and desire—I agree. Now are you telling me after I've done all of that I have to work too?*

Yep, that's exactly what I'm saying. The most beautiful philosophy in the world won't work if you won't. Education and motivation cover a lot of ground, but they won't cultivate any of it. Those just happen to be facts of life.

Even Adam and Eve had to tend the Garden of Eden. They were put there to work from the very beginning. We need to start teaching these facts about work early. Too often nowadays we expect our children to accomplish things, but then we turn around and give them everything—so there's no need for them to accomplish anything on their own in life. There's an ancient Jewish proverb that says if you don't teach children to work, you raise thieves. I believe there is some validity to that observation.

Speaking of education, William Bennett, the U.S. Secretary of Education from 1985-1988, in a *New York Times* article made this observation: "One of the unutterable truths of the education issue is that there is actually no correlation between funds expended on education and educational excellence." In other words, we have to do more than buy an education.

Education depends on motivation and the formation of good work habits.

Facts are facts. From 1960 to 1985, national expenditures on education nearly tripled—as SAT scores plummeted. Some of the most expensive public school systems in the country were among the least effective. The nation's parochial systems are cheap compared with their public counterparts. But who can doubt that they are more effective—as has been demonstrated time and again.

Education depends on motivation and the formation of good work habits. The most precise predictor of educational achievement is neither money nor class size—it is the quality of homework assigned and completed. All of this was well established most recently in the U.S. Education Department's publication, *What Works: Research about Teaching and Learning.* That's what they discovered.

I don't think we have an educational problem; I think we have a societal problem. We need to understand that even after we've invested billions of dollars in schools, we're still going to have to work in order to separate the information from the book it's in and put it into the minds of the students.

We need to teach students early—and learn this lesson ourselves—*you never work for somebody else.* Never. Somebody else might write your check and might sign your check. But the truth is, *you work for yourself,* as you're the one who eventually determines what amount they fill in on the check. We need to learn that and we need to teach it.

Every job is a self-portrait of the person who did it. Like the portrait painter who signs his or her name, we should autograph our work, any and every work, with excellence. When you do more than you're paid to do, you will eventually be paid more for what you do.

One of the great privileges I had was to learn important lessons as a child. My mother in the latter stages of her life often said that she deeply regretted that her children had to work so hard when we were children. Each one of us assured her repeatedly that one of the great benefits we had was the privilege of learning to work early on, and I think we finally persuaded her of that.

Every job is a self-portrait of the person who did it.

MORE WORK, MORE PAY

During the Great Depression years, I was a boy working in a grocery store in Yazoo City, Mississippi. Literally 90 to 95 percent of our business was done between about noon on Friday and eleven o'clock Saturday night. That's when the farmers came in and bought their supplies and all of the people who lived in town would get paid on Friday, so that's when they had money.

Because money was tight all around during that time, the boss only bought enough supplies that he thought he would sell that week. The stores back then didn't carry much inventory, so when the stores would run out of certain items, the store owners would ask to borrow from each other's inventory. A young fellow named Charlie Scott worked across the street; he was the runner for that store. I was the runner for our store.

Charlie flew through that front door of our store I'll bet ten thousand times. He'd run in and say to the owner, "Mr. Anderson, I need to borrow half a dozen cans of tomatoes." The boss would say, "Charlie, you know where they are. Go get them." Charlie would run back the aisle, snatch the six cans of tomatoes, run up to the counter, plop them down, scribble his name on the receipt Mr. Anderson had signed, then snatch up the tomato cans, and off he'd go in a dead run.

One day I asked Mr. Anderson, "Why is Charlie always in such a hurry?"

Mr. Anderson said, "Charlie is working for a raise; it looks like he's going to get it too."

"How do you know Charlie's gonna get a raise?"

Mr. Anderson grinned and said, "Charlie's going to get a raise because if the man he's working for doesn't give it to him, I am."

It is absolutely true that *when you do more than you're paid to do, you'll eventually be paid more for what you do.* Now the person you are working for might not, but somebody is going to see what you're doing, and they're going to give you the extra that you're going to deserve. It's not *pull* that makes the difference in life; it's *push* that makes the difference.

I'm convinced that one of the reasons the U.S. is suffering an import deficit today is because, for example, our Japanese counterparts are outworking us—not outperforming us, outworking us. The average Japanese high school graduate has been in the classroom more hours than the average American college graduate. The average Japanese student spends a little over three hours a day outside the classroom studying; the average American student spends a little less than thirty minutes a day outside the classroom studying. You can't persuade me that all of those hundreds of extra hours do not make a difference. They do. It's just a fact.

When you do more than you're paid to do, you'll eventually be paid more for what you do.

The Japanese are no smarter than we are, but they are working harder to accomplish their objectives. In Japan, if you ask average teenagers what university they will attend, what company and what department they will work for, what they will be doing in five years and ten years from today—they can tell you.

On the other hand, average American teenage boys can tell you how much money Michael Jackson got for the Pepsi commercial, how much money Herschel Walker got when he signed his Cowboy contract, how many records Bruce Springsteen has sold, and how many homeruns Reggie Jackson hit. But talk to them about the world of work, and you're talking about an entirely different situation. On average, they identify with the world of play.

Now don't misunderstand—that's not the kids' fault. We adults need to be the ones who are doing the working and the teaching, leading by example. We ought to teach our kids that they should do every job so enthusiastically and so well that, like Charlie Scott, they will advance from where they are to where they want to go.

I was at Mississippi State University conducting a seminar, and I told the Charlie Scott story. When the seminar was over, a fellow walked over to me and said, "When's the last time you've seen Charlie?" I told him it had been many years.

He said, "You probably wouldn't recognize him, would you?"

Probably the most humiliating thing anybody can do as far as a job is concerned is to lose one that they're overqualified for.

"No, I guess I wouldn't. It's been too long."

The man said, "Well, I didn't think so, because I'm Charlie Scott."

By then Charlie was a very wealthy man. He retired at age 50 to do exactly what he wanted to do in life. He was able to do that because what he learned as a kid in a grocery store, he applied throughout his work career. He always gave the extra effort and received the expected results.

GIVE IT YOUR BEST

Probably the most humiliating thing anybody can do as far as a job is concerned is to lose one that they're overqualified for. That often happens. They get a job that's absolutely beneath them and think, *I could go to sleep doing this,* and they generally do. When you get fired from a job you're overqualified for, what are you going to tell the next future employer? Are you going to say you were fired from a job that was putting sand in a bag and you couldn't handle it? Whatever the job is, the best way to qualify for the next one is to be super good at your current job.

A number of years ago my wife, our son, and I went to a steakhouse. After we were seated, a young busboy came over to the table and started pouring our water. He snatched up the first glass, doused it with water, picked up the next one and doused it, then picked up the last glass and doused it. I was watching him intently and the expression on his face was a sight to behold. When he finished, I asked, "You don't like your job?"

He grumbled, "No, I don't."

"Don't worry about it," I said. "You're not going to have it very long."

He looked at me in absolute shock and said, "What are you talking about?"

I said, "Young man, let me tell you something—with that attitude, I guarantee you're not going to have this job very long."

He did an abrupt turn around and walked through the door to the kitchen. He strode through the swinging door like he was mad at the world and then immediately pushed open the other door and walked back out with the biggest grin on his face—and what a dramatic difference it made!

Whatever the job—give it your best.

ENORMOUS SATISFACTION

No doubt you know the name Michael Landon. He acted in some incredible television series, including *Bonanza, Little House on the Prairie*, and *Highway to Heaven*. His first job was mixing glue and cutting ribbons in a ribbon factory. There's not much skill required to do that. But Michael Landon said he learned to give each job his absolute best, and when he gave it his best, he said that he got an enormous amount of satisfaction from it.

The way you get out of a job you don't like is to do it so extraordinarily well that nobody can afford to keep you in that position.

If you really want to get ahead, go to work early, which indicates an eagerness to get the job started. But if you stay late, that could signal that you simply couldn't finish the job. Be enthusiastic about your job and look for ways to learn more. Then when you've been with the company ten years, you have ten years' worth of experience, not one year's experience ten times—that's not the way you get promoted.

> **Anything worth doing is worth doing poorly—until you learn to do it well.**

My friend Steve Brown said, "Remember that anything worth doing is worth doing poorly—until you learn to do it well." Many times, we are hesitant to tackle something because we are uncertain of our skills. But when the employer, our boss, wants us to do something, we should say, "Sure, I'll give it my best shot. I've never done it before, but that doesn't mean I can't do it. I'll do my best to figure it out."

Consider the attitude of the old fella celebrating his hundredth birthday. Some smart aleck said, "Hey, Gramp, you gonna try for two hundred?" The man said, "Well, let's put it this way, I'm a lot stronger than I was on my first one." Some other smart aleck said, "Gramp, can you play the piano?" He said, "I don't know; I've never tried." I like his attitude.

Traditionally, people say they can't do this and can't do that. But how do they know if they've never tried? *If there's an opportunity—give it your best shot.* When you do the things you ought to do when you ought to do them, you will eventually be able to do the things you want to do when you want to do them.

The following principles are very significant:

- Do it now. If you have an assignment that you don't want to do, do it now—you'll get it done sooner and with less hassle. They'll probably praise you when you do. But if you delay starting, they will criticize you almost regardless of what happens as a result of you doing it.
- Stay with it. Persistence is important.

- Make failure your teacher not your undertaker—a detour is not a dead-end street.
- Learn to love your work. You can learn to love your work with an attitude adjustment. Look at your work as what you like to do and how you can improve whatever the job is.

For a number of years, Charles Kettering was a section foreman with General Motors. One day an out-of-work man came to him while he was on the job and asked Mr. Kettering for money for lunch. Mr. Kettering said, "No, I won't give you money for lunch, but I will take you to lunch." He took him to lunch and bought him a good meal. After lunch, the man said, "I'm not accustomed to begging, so I would like to work for you in order to pay you back for the meal." Mr. Kettering said, "All right. I have something for you to do." The job was to simply dig a hole in the ground that they had a need for right there.

Charles Kettering showed him how to dig a hole. He showed him exactly how to square it, how to make certain it was perfectly straight, and how to make it perfectly level. As Mr. Kettering was digging the hole, he was also demonstrating a considerable amount of pride in the way the hole was to be dug.

Then the man took over and he started working on the hole. He did a magnificent job. So good, in fact, that Mr. Kettering gave him a job. Later on, the man became a foreman and the man said, "Mr. Kettering, if anybody had shown me early in life the importance of doing a job well and taking pride in whatever I do, I never would have been without a job."

Work gives us more than a living; it gives us our life—our dignity and our destiny.

WORK AND LIFE

Work gives us more than a living; it gives us our life—our dignity and our destiny.

Years ago in the Smoky Mountains, several domestic hogs got loose and started living in the wild. Over a number of generations, the hogs got progressively wilder until they had so adjusted to the area that they were as wild as any hog could possibly be. Because they were very dangerous, the local people decided they needed to get rid of them, so they hired hunters. But the hogs were extraordinarily smart and eluded the hunters.

One day an old man showed up in the village there on the top of the mountainside. He had a donkey cart with some lumber in the back and some grain. He announced to the curious people around that he was going up on the mountain to catch the hogs. They kind of laughed at the old man, but he said, "Don't worry, I'll be back and let you know where I have the hogs trapped." About three weeks later, he came back down the mountain and told them where to find all the hogs enclosed in a pen.

"How on earth did you manage to do it?" they asked.

"Well, the first thing I did was simply lay the lumber out on the ground. Then I spread some of the grain on the ground. The old boar who was in charge was watching all of this from out in the woods and he led the sows and the little pigs out with him and they sniffed around. It took him a couple of hours before they were willing to take a bite of the grain, but it was there and it was good, and it was free—so they ate."

He continued, "The next day I went back and dug four post holes and put a post in each hole and then I put more grain right in the center. They were skeptical at first, but there was grain just like before. Over a period of about two weeks, I gradually built the fence up and set the trap door. Then I put a lot of grain inside the pen, and sure enough the lure of something for nothing—the free lunch—had captured them. They walked in and I sprung the lock on the gate. They were trapped."

To me, that story tells us a great deal about work and life. When you make a wild animal dependent upon people for food, you destroy its resourcefulness and the animal is in trouble.

The well-known saying is true: Give someone a fish and the person is fed for the day. But if you teach people to fish—to work for their food—they can feed themselves for life. When you give people handouts, you deny them their dignity and rob them of their destiny. We need to work to earn our way in life—and in doing so, we will reap the benefits of our effort.

BETWEEN THE GOALPOSTS

In your own written words, how would you describe the "wisdom of the ages" in a few sentences?

____

____

____

____

____

____

____

____

____

____

____

____

Fill in the blanks, and feel free to add words that come to mind:

Work is the ______________ of all business, the ______________ of all prosperity, and the ______________ of genius. Work can do more to ______________ youth than his or her own parents. Work is represented in the humblest ______________ and has laid the foundation of every ______________. Work is the ______________ that gives life its savor; but it must be ______________ before it can bestow its greatest ______________ and achieve its greatest ends. When ______________, work makes ______________ sweet, purposeful, and fruitful.

Are you a risk-taker? How about an opportunity-taker? Is there a difference between the two? How likely is it that you will grab hold of any potentially beneficial risk or opportunity that comes your way? Write your reasoning.

"Work gives us more than a living; it gives us our life—our dignity and our destiny." How true is this statement concerning your life as it is today? Will attaining the goals you set and working toward achieving those goals make this statement true?

BEYOND THE GOALPOSTS

Which true-life principles best represent your view of work:

____ Work is the foundation of all business.

____ Work is the source of all prosperity.

____ Work is the parent of genius.

____ Work teaches economics.

____ Work is the salt that gives life flavor.

____ Work is the price paid for success.

____ Work produces great blessings and achievements.

____ When loved, work makes life sweet, purposeful, and fruitful.

Have you ever fallen for a "something for nothing" scheme? How did it turn out?

What is your idea of a "dream job"?

____

How much "work" will it take to make that dream come true?

____

Do you have the required education? ________ Skills? ________ Dedication? ________

Commitment? ________ Desire? ________

At your current job, do you do more than is expected of you? Yes or No.

If you are a boss, do you notice employees who do more than what is expected of them? ________

When thinking seriously about your current job performance, how would you rate yourself from 1 to 10 if 10 is "Exceptional"? ________

What can you do to raise that number to 10 if not there already?

____

____

____

____

When on the job today, take notice of everything you do—and everything your boss does. If you want to advance, what goals do you need to set today to ***work*** toward moving up in your field?

____

____

____

____

Do you:

____ Go to work early to get a head start on the day?

____ Look for ways to learn more about your job/the company?

____ Exude eagerness to do a good job?

____ Go above and beyond your job description?

____ Get along with coworkers? Management?

____ Give each job your absolute best?

____ Feel satisfied at the end of the day knowing you earned your paycheck?

____ Look for opportunities to try something new?

____ Follow through immediately on assignments when asked?

____ Give praise where praise is due to coworkers?

____ Think of work as a privilege, something to value and appreciate?

If true that "you never work for somebody else" and that "you work for yourself," what kind of worker will you be? Lazy, incompetent, grouchy, absent-minded, and disrespectful? Of course not. List the characteristics of the kind of worker you will be for yourself, which in reality will be the worker you should be in your everyday workplace:

When you leave work and travel home, do you most often feel proud of your day's work? Were you as productive as possible? Were your coworkers glad that they spent the workday with you? Did your boss smile when he passed by? If you answered ***yes*** to each of the questions, good for you! You're on a wonderful journey to reaching your goals and success!

CHAPTER 7

THE BEST JOB EVER

CHANGE your attitude about your job from something you *have* to do to something you *get* to do. If you change your attitude, there will be a big difference in your performance.

A few years ago, my son and I were returning from Phoenix after the Christmas holiday. I had for several years been going there to play in the Fellowship of Christian Athletes Pro-Am Golf Tournament. My son had played with me this time and we were enthused and excited and had a lot of fun.

As we walked up to the gate agent and I placed our tickets on the counter, I said to the agent, "Hi! How're you doing?"

"Compared to what?" he said, grumbling.

I smiled and said, "Well, compared to the all the people who unlike you do not have a magnificent job with a wonderful company living in America and the free enterprise system where you enjoy all of the freedoms that life has to offer, with a marvelous opportunity to get ahead on the job you have and render a real service to other people, and enjoying good health all at the same time! So, how're you doing?"

If you change your attitude, there will be a big difference in your performance.

The gate agent grinned from ear to ear and said, "I'm doing a whole lot better than I was one minute ago!" Interestingly, he moved both of us up to first class! When you realize there are millions of people who don't get to do a job, then it's easy to put your own job in the proper perspective.

ARE YOU KIDDING ME?

I love the story of the two ladies who had grown very disgruntled with their jobs. According to them, they were miserable and unhappy to say the least. They decided they had enough and were going to quit the next Friday afternoon. Thursday night they got together to plan for the next day. They decided to go in early the next morning, dress neatly for their last day, clean up the kitchen and the area around, get everything spick-and-span, make the coffee, and then when the early workers started arriving, they would make it a point to serve each one a cup of coffee and be very gracious and kind and pleasant with them.

When the first unsuspecting employee walked in, one of the women greeted the lady and said, "Well, good morning! I had no idea you came in this early. My, you look nice today. Come on in. I made a pot of coffee. Sit down. I want to serve it for you."

The lady was flabbergasted because she knew the woman and knew what kind of attitude she usually had. So she thanked her profusely and told her how much she really appreciated this early morning greeting. Another worker walked in and they gave that person the same treatment. Then the third, fourth, and so on.

Then the first customer came in and one of the women greeted the customer enthusiastically, saying, "You're our first customer today and I can already tell we're going to have a wonderful day because I'll bet everybody is going to be just like you—pleasant and cheerful and friendly." The customer looked absolutely astonished and said, "Well my goodness! Thank you very much. I really appreciate being greeted this way!"

All day long the women went on like that. About 4 o'clock in the afternoon there was a breather in customer traffic and the two ladies got together for a quick chat. One said to the other, "When are you going to tell them? Or do you want me to tell them?"

And the other one said, "What are you talking about?"

"You know, who's going to tell them we're going to quit today?"

"Quit the best job I ever had? Are you kidding me?"

As I understand it, that is literally a true story. When you change your attitude about your job, it will make a dramatic difference in your performance on the job. What you do *off* the job plays a major part in how far you go *on* the job.

What you do **off** the job plays a major part in how far you go **on** the job.

DEMAND MORE OF YOURSELF

Another principle is to be demanding of yourself. Basketball coach John Wooden of UCLA said there is no great fun, satisfaction, or joy derived from doing something that's easy. Failure is not fatal, but failure to change might be.

Coach Wooden was the most successful basketball coach in history. He never had a losing season; won ten of twelve national championships at UCLA, seven of them in a row. Wooden said that he considered players' morals just as carefully as he considered their quickness.

We need to understand that effort is the key, but direction and loyalty are paramount. It makes no sense to do a super job on what you should not be doing at all. Efficiency is doing things right. Effectiveness is doing the right things efficiently. Hard work plus traditional values are the winning combination.

100 percent of them said that hard work was the key to their success.

At Korn Ferry International, in conjunction with the UCLA School of Management, they did a study of 1,361 vice presidents who had an average income of $215,000. The most successful ones had been on their jobs more than fifteen years and they had only held two jobs. Also, 87 percent of them were still married to their one and only mate; 89 percent of them had two, three, four, or more children; 71 percent said integrity was their most important asset; and 100 percent of them said that *hard work was the key to their success.*

U.S. News and World Report, the January 13, 1986 issue, discussed the one million millionaires in the United States. Twenty to thirty years had been the average length of time they took to acquire their fortune, and they earned their money by supplying basic human needs. As mentioned before but worth repeating—less than 1 percent of the millionaires in the U.S. earned their money in music, radio, television, movies, entertainment, or athletics. All of those put together, less than 1 percent had earned their money in all of those fields combined. That is worth pondering.

The Honorable Clarence Pendleton, Chairman of the U.S. Commission on Civil Rights from 1981-1988, personally told me that as a result of studies they had done—particularly in the black community where there's been so many false hopes raised about how to get to the top in athletics, music, and entertainment—the odds are one thousand times as great that a young black athlete will become a successful doctor or a lawyer as they are that he will become a professional athlete.

When you start thinking about what you read in the last chapter about desire, that's one of the reasons I told the story about the young man who had an overwhelming desire to be a light heavyweight champion, and yet he failed—because he didn't have the skills or the experience. I believe that if we start aiming our young people at goals, they have a thousand times as good a chance of getting there, and we will have rendered our country and the young people a much greater service.

A Lewis Harris poll of people who had an income of $142,000 a year or more and had a net worth in excess of a half million dollars, not including their home, described these successful people as being:

- Unexciting
- Middle-aged
- Cautious
- Stress family values and the work ethic
- 83 percent were married
- 96 percent acquired their net worth through hard work
- 80 percent are politically conservative or middle-of-the-road
- Relatively nonmaterialistic
- Major objective was to provide for their family—85 percent said that was the major objective
- 11 percent rated owning an expensive car as being a high priority
- Prestige and the badges of success don't matter as much as family, education, and their business or job

Not much excitement—but lots of happiness. These successful people have a good standard of living; but infinitely more important, they have an excellent quality of life. *Persistent, consistent, disciplined hard work makes the difference.*

HARD WORK MAKES THE DIFFERENCE

Thomas Edison is often thought of as being the predominant inventive genius of our country's history. In fact, he had many successful inventions, especially when you consider all of the work that he did; it's easy to understand why he was so successful. You may have heard the story about how a young reporter came to him one time and said, "Mr. Edison, I understand you have been working on one experiment ten thousand times." This was during his efforts to invent the incandescent light.

Mr. Edison said, "That's right."

The reporter asked, "How does it feel to have failed ten thousand times?"

Mr. Edison said, "Young man, you're just getting started in life, so let me tell you this...and please don't ever forget it. I have not failed ten thousand times. I have successfully found ten thousand ways that will not work."

It's the difference in your attitude that counts.

When Jerry West, one of the all-time great basketball players in the NBA, was a youngster, he was so bad that the kids on the playground would not even let him play with them. When in the school gym, he used to lag behind the other boys, and after everyone left and had turned off the lights, Jerry would stay behind and shoot baskets in the shadows. He didn't have access to the light switches, so he spent hour after hour just barely able to make out the outline of the basket. He eventually developed the touch for hitting that basket almost in complete darkness. That's the reason he went on to become one of the all-time shooting guards in the history of the NBA. It takes a lot of effort to reach your goals.

My friend Joel Weldon tells a story that I think has so much merit. The Chinese plant a seed to raise a bamboo tree. They water and fertilize that seed the first year, but nothing happens. The second, third, and fourth years they do the same—they water and fertilize it, but nothing happens. The fifth year they water and fertilize that seed again, and sometime during the course of the fifth year, in a period of roughly six weeks, the Chinese bamboo tree grows roughly 90 feet high. The questions are—did it grow 90 feet in six weeks or did it grow 90 feet in five years? The answer is obvious. Had there been any year when they did not water and fertilize it, there would have been no Chinese bamboo tree.

Many times we work and work and work and nothing happens. We work again and nothing happens, and then we give that final effort and succeed. You have probably seen it happen when all of a sudden someone becomes an overnight success. You may have experienced that yourself in some area of your life. Yet what others don't see is all the work and effort that was done beforehand that actually led to that "overnight success." I've heard it said that *failure is the line of least resistance—success occurs when opportunity meets preparation.* I believe that's true.

> Failure is the line of least resistance—success occurs when opportunity meets preparation.

PERSISTENCE AND DETERMINATION

One of the most intriguing stories I've heard is the story of Demosthenes. You may recognize the name as the great Greek orator who scaled oratorical heights that they say have never been equaled. When Demosthenes was a young man, there was a law on the books that the inheritance left by a person's father could be challenged by anyone in public debate. If the challenger won the debate, the heir could literally win their fortune. Demosthenes had a speech difficulty; he was also very shy and awkward.

During the debate, Demosthenes was embarrassed and humiliated. Not only did he lose all of his self-respect, he also lost his family fortune. But he did not lose his will and his determination. He went to the seashore and placed pebbles in his mouth and he stood there for hours and days projecting his voice as he spoke into the waves and the wind. Over a period of time, by being an excellent student and an extraordinarily hard worker, he became famous the world over for his oratorical skills. History didn't record the name of the man who stole Demosthenes's fortune, but Demosthenes has been remembered kindly for several centuries.

U.S. President Calvin Coolidge put it this way: "Nothing in the world can take the place of persistence. Talent will not; nothing is more common than unsuccessful men with talent. Genius will not; unrewarded genius is almost a proverb. Education will not; the world is full of educated derelicts. Persistence and determination alone are omnipotent."

"Nothing in the world can take the place of persistence."

Vince Lombardi, the legendary coaching genius who was the only man to ever coach three consecutive World Championship football teams, said, "I've never known a man worth his salt who in the long run deep down in his heart did not appreciate the grind and the discipline." There is something in good people that truly yearns for and needs discipline.

World famous cellist Pablo Casals, long after he had achieved international recognition as an artist, still practiced six hours every day. Someone asked him why the continued effort. His reply was simply, "I think I'm making progress."

The opportunity for greatness doesn't knock—it's inside each one of us. However, we must work to get it out. We are often told to "Strike while the iron is hot," which is good advice. Better advice, however, is to make the iron hot by striking. Yes, persistence pays off. Life is tough. It's not where you start but when you finish that makes the difference—a big difference.

Harry Conn, in his beautiful book *The Four Trojan Horses of Humanism,* writes about the book *Who's Who of America.* That's different from *Who's Who in America,* which is a directory that provides information about leaders and achievers. In this book they discover that it takes 25,000 laboring families to produce one member of *Who's Who in America.* It takes 5,000 lawyers to produce one member of *Who's Who* in their families. Of 2,500 dentists, they will produce one family member who will be a member of *Who's Who.*

Yet it takes only seven Christian missionary families to produce one member of *Who's Who.* I wondered why. As I reflected on that statistic, the predominant reason comes down to five factors:

1. Of all the people on the face of this earth, missionaries have to have the most faith.
2. They have to struggle their hardest under the most difficult circumstances.
3. They have to learn how to get along with strange people in a strange land, learning ingenuity.
4. They have to be able to really work and improvise and sacrifice.
5. They have to learn how to deal with frustrations and heartbreak and disappointments and defeats and setbacks.

> Life is tough. It's not where you start but when you finish that makes the difference—a big difference.

When you put all of those factors together, the end results are absolutely magnificent.

No, it's not easy to reach your goals. I haven't even hinted that it was going to be easy, because it's not. But the rewards are absolutely tremendous.

AN OLD CHROME-PLATED PUMP

I honestly believe that if you didn't really catch anything you've read up until right now, if you get the message in the following pump story, I believe this alone is going to be worth your time.

A good friend of mine, Bernard Haygood, and his brother-in-law, Jimmy Glen, were out riding in the South Alabama foothills one brutally hot August day and they got thirsty. Bernard pulled his car behind an old, abandoned farmhouse and they saw an old pump. They hopped out of the car ran over to the pump and Bernard grabbed the handle and started to pump it.

After a couple of minutes, he said, "Jimmy, get that old bucket over there and go get some water out of the creek. We're going to have to prime the pump before we get any water to come out."

They primed the pump but still no water. After another few minutes, Bernard said, "You know Jimmy, I don't believe there's any water down there." Jimmy said, "I think there is. You see, in South Alabama, the wells are deep. We're glad they are because the deeper the well, the cooler, the cleaner, the sweeter, the purer, and the better tasting the water is."

"...the deeper the well, the cooler, the cleaner, the sweeter, the purer, and the better tasting the water is."

That's pretty much the way it is in life, isn't it. Isn't it true that the things we have to work the hardest for are the things that have the most value? Isn't it true that the promotion we really have to hustle to get means the most to us? Isn't it true that the subject that's the most difficult to learn we appreciate the most when we know it? Isn't it true that the gal or the guy who is the most difficult to get to notice us is the one we get the most excited about?

Back to the story, Bernard kept pumping and pumping—wondering how much work he was willing to do in order to get a drink of water. Finally, Bernard threw up his hands and said, "Jimmy, I just don't believe there's any water down there." Jimmy said, "Don't stop! When you stop, the water goes all the way back down, and then we have to start all over."

There are a couple of magnificent lessons for us already in that story. First of all, in order to get some water out, you have to put something in—you have to prime the pump. So many people stand in front of the woodstove of life and say, "Nice stove, give me some heat and then I'll put some wood in you." Many times an employee goes to the employer and says, "Give me a raise and then I'll start coming to work on time." Many times the student will say, "Teacher, I know I haven't studied this semester and I know I really haven't done well, but if I take a failing grade home, my mom's going to be really disappointed. Give me a good grade this time, Teacher. And if you do, I promise I'll read and study next semester."

What they're really saying is, reward me and then I'll perform. But it doesn't work that way; if it did, can you just imagine a farmer saying, "Lord, you know I didn't plant anything this year, but if you give me a good crop, next year I'll plant more than anybody."

That's not the way life works. You have to put something in before you can expect to get something out—and then you have to do a whole lot of pumping. And if you ever stop, all that good effort is lost.

Jimmy grabbed the handle of that old pump and he started pumping and pumping. He worked hard at pumping, giving it all of his effort. Then once the water started to flow, all he had to do was keep steady pressure on it and they ended up getting more water than they knew what to do with.

You have to put something in before you can expect to get something out.

Did you ever notice that when things are good, they get better? And when they're bad, they get worse? Those times have nothing whatsoever to do with what's going on out there. Rather, it has everything to do with what's going on between your ears.

The basic problem most people have is that when they get involved in a new project they say, "Well, I'll just give this project my attention for a bit and if it works out that's good, and if it doesn't work out that's okay too. Nothing ventured nothing gained." With that kind of attitude, nothing is going to happen.

But when you first get involved and you really go after it—you pump and pump and pump—then you will make progress; and once you get into the flow, then all you have to do is keep a good, steady pressure on it and you will reap results.

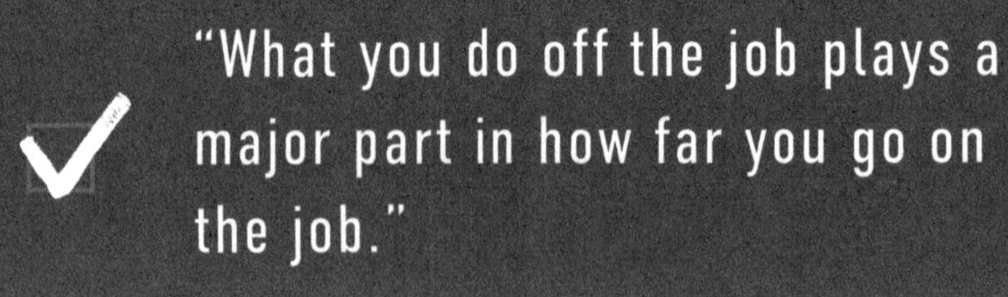

You know what I like about these facts-of-life principles to reach your goals? I like that each one has nothing to do with your age or education, nothing to do with whether you're black or white or older or young or male or female or extrovert or introvert, well-educated or uneducated.

These principles simply provide ways for free people to succeed. It is our God-given right to work—to work as long and as hard as we wish and as enthusiastically as we wish to accomplish our objectives in life. I believe that is what the United States of America is all about. Be persistent, determined, and keep working—if you do, you will accomplish your goals.

BETWEEN THE GOALPOSTS

What difference would it make if you went to work tomorrow with a bright and cheery attitude? Would your coworkers notice? Your boss? The people at the cafeteria? The cleaning staff? The repairperson? Anyone you see during the day? Visualize their reactions and choose tomorrow to start the day with a smile for everyone you meet—at work and at home. Chances are they will return the smile every time.

"What you do off the job plays a major part in how far you go on the job." What activity or activities are you involved in off the job? Does it reflect your desires in life, your goals, your talents, your best qualities? If you have no activities outside of work, make a list of things you would like to do to enhance, round out, or balance your life. Take steps to incorporate one or two of those activities.

It is true that what you work for the hardest is what will have the most value in your life. Think of your last achievement—something you strove for and finally received. Did that memory bring a smile to your face? Now think of all the good feelings you will have when you put to work all of what you learned throughout this book and you obtain your objective by reaching your goals in life. Good times ahead!

BEYOND THE GOALPOSTS

Write the first five things that come to mind that you ***like*** about your current job:

1. ______
2. ______
3. ______
4. ______
5. ______

Write the first five things that come to mind when you think about your dream job:

1. ______
2. ______
3. ______
4. ______
5. ______

Do you see any similarities?

______

______

If you changed your attitude about your current job to reflect gratitude for having a job, how different would your daily grind be?

Define what "traditional values" mean to you:

Do you consider these values:

Very Important Important Somewhat Important Not Important

If you answered Not Important, list what values you consider Very Important:

Food for thought:

- Realizing there are no "overnight successes," how many years are you willing to work hard to reach your goals?
- How many "fun" activities are you willing to give up to make that last call to a potential client?
- How many nights are you willing to stay at the office to meet a deadline?
- How persistent and determined are you when pursuing your goal(s)?
- How prepared are you to grab onto an opportunity that is right around the corner?

To drive home the point that ***you must give something to get something,*** make up 3-4 scenarios along the lines of the book's examples: "Nice stove, give me some heat and then I'll put some wood in you." And "Give me a raise and then I'll start coming to work on time."

It's a fact that if you work hard at something you will appreciate it more than if someone gives it to you. For instance, many heirs waste their inheritance. And many lottery winners waste the winnings. On the other hand, putting a delicious from-scratch meal on the table, completing an especially challenging assignment at work, and earning an A in a hard class bring a deep-down satisfaction that lasts longer than momentary financial pleasures. Write about some of those deep-down pleasures you've experienced over the years:

Right now, what projects can you take on with more gusto, more focus, and more effort to reap the reward of a "job well done!"

According to a 2018 survey, the following are seven traits of successful executives[1]:

1. Made learning a priority throughout their career.

2. Worked hard at each job while climbing the ladder.

3. Practiced servant leadership (humble and helpful to others).

4. Pursued the best opportunities available (local or relocating if necessary).

5. Steady and consistent work history.

6. Quality online profile.

7. Aware of their strengths and value.

Of these seven traits, how many are currently part of your career life? If not all, when will you begin to infiltrate each into your journey to reach your goals?

Are you progressing daily toward reaching your goals? Or are you stagnant? ______________

Do you need to be goaded by others to follow your set path toward success? If so, stop and reconsider that path. Perhaps over the years your desires have changed, maybe your family situation is different, or your health has made a significant impact on your progress. It's never too late to readjust your goals. "The opportunity for greatness doesn't knock—it's inside each one of us."

Write your thoughts and then take appropriate action to accomplish your heart's desire—reach out for whatever you choose your destiny to be. (You may want to read this book from the beginning again, reworking all of the steps mentioned—beginning with the "Wild Ideas" list!)

____

____

____

____

____

____

____

____

Nothing can stop you from reaching your goals but you! "Be persistent, determined, and keep working—if you do, you will accomplish your goals."

NOTE

1. Rebecca Bosl, "Seven Traits of Successful Executives (And How You Can Be Successful Too), ***Forbes,*** April 27, 2018; https://www.forbes.com/sites/forbescoachescouncil/2018/04/27/seven-traits-of-successful-executives-and-how-you-can-be-successful-too/?sh=716de98243e9; accessed December 18, 2020.

ABOUT THE AUTHOR

ZIG ZIGLAR (1926-2012) was one of America's most influential and beloved encouragers and believers that everyone could be, do, and have more. He was a motivational speaker, teacher, and trainer who traveled extensively delivering messages of humor, hope, and encouragement. His appeal transcended age, culture, and occupation. From 1970 until 2010, Zig traveled more than five million miles around the world sharing powerful life-improvement messages, cultivating the energy of change.

Zig Ziglar wrote more than thirty celebrated books on personal growth, leadership, sales, faith, family, and success. He was a committed family man, dedicated patriot, and an active church member. His unique delivery style and powerful presentations earned him many honors, and today he is still considered one of the most versatile authorities on the science of human potential.

www.soundwisdom.com